The Dybbuk
of Delight

The Dybbuk of Delight

*an anthology of
Jewish women's poetry*

*(ed) by Sonja Lyndon
and Sylvia Paskin*

Five Leaves Publications
in association with the European Jewish Publications Society

The Dybbuk of Delight

Published in 1995 by Five Leaves Publications
PO Box 81, Nottingham NG5 4ER, in association with the
European Jewish Publications Society.

Designed & set by 4 Sheets Design & Print
Printed in Great Britain by Antony Rowe

ISBN 0 907123 57 0

Five Leaves Publications
acknowledge financial assistance for this collection
from East Midlands Arts

Errata

P.11 - 2nd last line should read
Jane Liddell-King's . . .

P.115 - 8th line of poem should read
I want to hear you talking

CONTENTS

1

4

INTRODUCTION

"I am the dybbuk of delight
I slip into the souls of those who need me"

The title for this anthology has been taken from these two lines in a poem by Michelene Wandor entitled "Lilith's Dance". The phrase "dybbuk of delight" appealed to us for a number of reasons: the paradoxical notion of a dybbuk as a positive force struck us as suitably provocative and transgressive for a book that was breaking new ground, by being the first ever publication of Jewish women's poetry in this country; and the celebratory note struck by the coupling of the word "dybbuk" with that of "delight", sat well with our feeling that this was indeed something to be celebrated.

Many people will only have come across the term "dybbuk" in association with Anski's play of the same name, first produced in Poland in 1920 and recently revived by the Royal Shakespeare Company. A dybbuk is by definition a wandering soul who, having failed to gain entry through the gates of gehinnom (purgatory) is doomed to wander the earth helplessly, its sole possibility of salvation being to enter the body of a living person. Only by possessing someone through whose deeds refinement can take place, can a dybbuk qualify for favourable divine judgement. Exorcism, as in Anski's play, is the alternative means of rehabilitation.

In our research into the meaning and manifestation of dybbuks, we were struck by two things: first that the impure spirit only cleaves (the term "dybbuk" comes from the Hebrew for cleaving or clinging) to someone who desires to cleave unto them; secondly, that "possession" takes place in a moment of melancholia or confusion.

These two conditions for spiritual possession struck us very forcibly as being highly analogous to the act of creative writing. Not only does the muse, the act of inspiration, only come to us when we are in some unconscious state of readiness and acceptance, when we desire to cleave unto it, but, for the poet in particular, this act very often takes place in a moment of confusion or melancholy.

For us then, "the dybbuk of delight" is the creative muse, who slips into the souls of those who need her, and who speaks through us in a voice that we sometimes fail to recognise, but that we cannot deny.

Equally fitting, we felt, for this first anthology of *Jewish women's poetry* was the fact that the title comes from a poem about Lilith, the first woman to appear on the Jewish historical stage. Lilith, the precursor of Eve, has been reclaimed by Jewish feminists, who have sought to dispel her image as the malevolent spirit and sexual harridan, as the creature who preys on men in their sleep causing nocturnal emissions, and as the slayer of new-born babies, a vengeful spirit against whom protection must be sought in the form of amulets. Centuries of malign commentary by male scholars and rabbis have either obscured or overlaid the story of Lilith, whose name cannot be found in the central canon of Jewish scripture, namely the Torah, having been relegated to more esoteric writings such as the Zohar, a Kabbalistic work of the thirteenth century, as well as being found in the writings of the Talmud.

Lilith like Adam, was formed from dust or earth, but having been created his equal she refused to lie beneath him for the sexual act. When Adam threatened to overpower her, she dared to utter the ineffable name of God, and fled, or in some accounts was banished, to the wilderness. Lilith is therefore that quality in woman that refuses to be bowed in a relationship, she is the primeval, instinctual, free spirit of woman. For the male Jewish sages she represented the bitterness of the rejected female, hence her sexual stalking of the sleeping man and her vengeful slaying of the newborn child. Over the centuries a composite image was built up that included the fornicating harlot, the long-haired demon of the night - the name Lilith is closely connected with the Hebrew "laylah" for night - and the demon of screeching - the letters of her name add up to form the word "screech", according to the kabbalistic practice of gematriah.

For the late twentieth century feminist, however, this depiction of a screeching woman is all too reminiscent of the familiar male put down of an assertive and forceful woman as "shrill". It is a negative reaction to a woman's attempt at being heard.

Not only have Jewish feminists sought to redeem Lilith, championing her rebelliousness towards Adam, and her determination to be heard, but other twentieth century figures such as Jung have made positive references to her, calling her a shamanistic anima. However the forces of both Eve, mother of all living things and of Lilith are evidenced in the central conflict that besets women, namely the conflict between giving birth and nurture, and needing to produce and nourish ideas and work . Never before has this conflict been so forefronted for the daughters of Lilith and Eve as in the late twentieth century. The battle between these two forces was already building up at the beginning the century as is brilliantly illustrated by Virginia Woolf in her description of the Angel in the House:

"....I discovered that...I should do battle with a certain phantom. And the phantom was a woman and when I came to know her better I called her after the heroine of a famous poem, "The Angel in the House"...She was intensely sympathetic. She was immensely charming. She was utterly unselfish. She excelled in the difficult arts of family life. if there was a chicken, she took the leg; if there was a draught,

she sat in it. In short she was so constituted that she never had a mind or a wish of her own, but preferred to sympathise with the minds and wishes of others. Above all, I need not say it - she was pure...And when I came to write, I encountered her with the very first words. the shadow of her wings fell upon my page; I heard the rustling of her skirts in the room. She slipped behind me and whispered...be sympathetic; be tender; flatter; deceive; use all the arts and wiles of your sex. Never let anyone guess you have a mind of your own. Above all be pure. And she made as if to guide my pen. I now record the one act for which I take some credit to myself...I turned upon her and caught her by the throat. I did my best to kill her. My excuse, if I were to be had up in a court of law, should be that I acted in self defense. Had I not killed her, she would have killed me."
("Professions for Women" from "Death of the Moth and Other Essays.")

For the Jewish woman, the Angel of the House has been a particularly potent force - if there was a chicken she indeed took the pulka! - and was expected to excel in "the arts of family life" while remaining both invisible and silent in the public domain of synagogue and communal affairs. The injunction against the sound of a woman's singing voice is still adhered to in orthodox services, and recalls the ancient fear of Lilith, the siren who could distract and tempt men away from their serious purpose.

The cultural weight that has for so long imposed both invisibility and silence on Jewish women has been lifted in the second half of the twentieth century. Jewish women today have been freed by feminism, by increasing secularisation or by more enlightened forms of Judaism to express themselves in a way never before possible. This anthology is a testament to these liberating forces. It was seeded in Autumn of 1992 when Sonja guest-edited an issue of the

Jewish Quarterly sub-titled "Images and Voices of Jewish Women", an issue that attracted the attention of Five Leaves Publications and led to the commissioning of this book. Initially, we thought only in terms of an international anthology, as we imagined it would be highly unlikely that we would find enough poets here in Britain - Sylvia recalled wanting to edit an anthology of writing on contemporary aspects of the Ten Commandments, but when she approached several established Jewish writers, many of them wrote back and declined, as they did not wish to be considered as British-Jewish writers. British Jews have been notoriously covert about their Jewish identity unlike their American counterparts.

How gloriously wrong we were! Poems poured in from all corners of the British Isles - even as far as Jersey - and we were so impressed by the quality of the British poets that we decided to concentrate on these submissions. We felt this was living proof of how many women were writing within these shores, and with what commitment and enthusiasm. This anthology provided an excellent and long overdue opportunity to bring them under one roof. Their presence here will hopefully give rise to other publications of this kind with the richness, imagination and intensity one experiences here.

However, we have included the poetry of some women living abroad - some of whom are British-born. These poets have been included because they reflect on sometimes similar and sometimes engagingly 'other' views of Jewish women's experience, which serve as a counter-point to those from the British Isles - after all, how could we resist Anne Ranasinghe's:

"................... I open the door
to the moon-washed garden - such stillness under the golden light

of the huge Poya moon, all branches and leaves immobile -
searching for Atteriya, Queen of the Night."

Overall, this anthology reflects the interests of contemporary Jewish women both sacred and profane. As one might
expect there are historical themes - the problem of assimilation as in Sue Hubbard's poignant evocation of "belonging"
in "Inheritance" and "Assimilation". Emigration is another
important historical theme as in Lotte Kramer's "Dead
Rhine" and "The Non-Emigrant" or Gerda Mayer's poem
"The Emigration Game". Lotte Kramer writes:"It was only
in my middle years that I began to write mainly from a
sense of isolation and transplantation which brought back
that earlier event when I came to England with a
"Kindertransport" in 1939. A traumatic experience."

Jewish festivals and themes are explored in several of the
poems - Linda Parkes' "Seder Eve", Janet Berenson-
Perkins' poem "The Eternal Light", which is about the
Sabbath: " .....threads of prayer song rise from hibernation,
lace-winged by imperfect memory"; Rabbi Elizabeth Sarah's
"Meditation for Tefillin" and Valerie Sinason's "Passover" -
"What a way to make a family eat together - Curses, bitter
herbs and chicken soup..." and of course other poems about
food some of which are straightforward, some political and
some downright subversive - Miriam Halahmy's "Making
Kubeh" and "Washing Apples", Myra Schneider's "Root
Vegetable Stew", Wanda Barford's "Beetroot" and Joan
Ballin's excoriating poem "Vienna, Sweet City of My
Dreams" on the ramifications of sachertorte from "thin
black icing..." to the ashes of the Holocaust.

The Holocaust features in a number of the poems and it was
a theme which we had to wrestle with in terms of balance
and weight, since it makes painful and disturbing reading -
Joan Liddell-King's searingly unforgettable "Science and
Industry" comes to mind. The Holocaust is the wound from

which we can never recover and to which we must return and pick and probe over and over again in a fruitless effort to discover its terrible significance. This revisiting is not vicarious or self-indulgent. It enables us to grieve and mourn and pay homage in poems such as "Bone Woman" by Gloria Tessler, Wanda Barford's "Family Snaps", Thilde Fox's "Inheritance" and Leah Thorn's extraordinary and shocking "Holocaust Junkie".

Our inability and unwillingness to escape from this theme is expressed succinctly by Tricia Corob: "As individuals as well as collectively, we have to deal with inheritance of trauma in this century. But more anciently too, we have memories of homelessness and exile. I think the most creative use of pain is to allow it to release resources of compassion for other people and other races." Hilde Schiff, who herself has recently edited an anthology of Holocaust poetry, has some additional important insights: "Writing poetry on the subject of the Holocaust is characteristically difficult and complex. The subjects contemplated are in themselves emotion-laden. The poet's attitude towards them may be composed of many layers and even remain unresolved in the end. And such poetic expertise as is brought to bear upon the material of the poem must always be spiritually suspect: is one exploiting matters that are, or should be, untouchable? Or in creating an autonomous literary object out of them, is one attempting to wrest from the wasteland of the Shoah some small atom that could count as a victory over it."

There are also poems of a more joyous nature, affirming love in all its guises - for lovers, for friends, for children, for uncles, for aunts and for parents and grandparents; there are poems that affirm reverence for artists such as Lucian Freud, Egon Schiele, Marc Chagall and Rembrandt and writers such as Virginia Woolf, Colette, Annette von Droste-Hülshoff. As would be expected in such an anthology, there are poems that touch on the varied aspects of women's lives not just the life cycle of birth and marriage, menstruation, menopause but also themes of incest, childlessness and ageing, as well as the quotidian serendipity of life.

The poets span a broad spectrum of Jewish identity to include the observant Jew, the converted Jew, the half-Jew, and the assimilated Jew. Everyone can find themselves here in some form. Jewish identity is a theme in itself that was addressed by some of our poets in their poetry and in their correspondence with us on the nature and scope of this anthology. One or two poets declined our invitation to be part of this anthology, disliking the very notion of being pigeon-holed by race or gender. Fran Landesman preferred to see herself as "an androgynous time-traveller", stating firmly:

"I don't want to be a woman
I don't want to be a man
I don't want to be a Jew
Or a Pres-byt-er-ian..."

(from "Me")

Others like Joan Michelson shared with us the challenge of definition: "I've been turning over in my head the issue of oblique and frontal responses to the grouping "Jewish Women". Women are fairly easy to identify, but who is Jewish? Looking through my poems for even an oblique connection, I saw that there were very few and that American and English literary culture, despite a much wider reading and a particular interest in Israeli literature as well as literature of the Holocaust have provided the major models and been the major influences in language and subject. Beyond this, English culture in particular with its long practised language, modes and manner of partial concealment has diverted, if not concealed my voice...Each of us is Jewish within a particular culture and greatly influenced by that culture. Each if us is Jewish to a different degree and the Jewish connection carries a different degree of compulsion and significance for each of us."

Alix Pirani writes of her work: "I see myself expressing that acute tension between bounded safety and unbounded passion that women and Jews experience in this British culture."

For Elizabeth Sarah, this tension was expressed at a young age in the schism between the writing she did from the "head" - mostly academic papers - and the writing she did from the "heart" - mostly poems. This changed with the arrival of feminism in the late seventies, when she learned to replace "objectivity" with "a passionate pursuit of wholeness and personal integrity". Along with other writers in this anthology she shared with us her writing process: "I don't actually write my poems - at least that is not how I begin the process of composition. Each poem forms itself inside me whole, in response to an intense experience/emotion. Then, once I recognise the words, I sit down and write. It is at this point that the technician inside me gets to work on the fine-tuning - refining, modifying, - shaping the words on the page. The process ends with a final internal drafting once again, until the words - repeated over and over - feel completely true and I am content to commit my recitation to paper. The crucial thing is that my heart is speaking. The writing is a secondary function." Referring to the composition of her poem "Meditation for Tefillin" she was gazing into the abyss of the future after a period of loss in her life, when "I felt my heart/soul flutter and as the feeling became a Presence hovering around me, a fragile bridge of words began to form inside me and to span the void."

Valerie Sinason also gives us a fascinating insight into the creative process:

14

"Ever since I was a child, the creation of a poem has always followed the same sequence. I have to be in a reflective mood, aware of a sense of loss over something internal or external. This "incubating" period can take a few days or a few weeks. After a while I am consciously aware I am in the mood that provides the environment for a poem. I wonder what the poem will be, what word will present itself in my mind. I have a feeling of excitement and anticipation. Also I know that my unconscious has succeeded in resolving something, in allowing a thought and a word passage from its depth into my consciousness.

Suddenly, day or evening, alone in my study or in company, a single word or phrase comes into my head. Whatever I am doing waits, while I properly greet this awaited guest. Although the poem is my poem and the words are my words, the beginning of a poem is always experienced as a guest from elsewhere. Once I have received the first words I long for a period of two to three hours to get to my computer or pen and paper, if I am not at home, and follow where those words take me.

I love the process of shaping the words and sounds that follow. When a line comes into my head I feel in touch with a sense of beauty. I experience the separate words I think of, as aesthetic objects. To have a mind that can play with words is something I appreciate enormously. Usually after two to three hours I am satisfied. My poems are rarely longer than 40 lines and that period allows me to write and re-write. After that I need to wait a week to see if I think the poem is a raw and primary process or whether it is a finished poem. When I have just written it I always find it beautiful! I write between 8-12 poems a year and my output has never been more. If I try to write a poem before a line has visited me it is always raw."

The "guest from elsewhere" is surely none other than our

"dybbuk of delight", a spirit that cannot be at rest until it has found expression, a spirit that takes us over, and by whom we become possessed. What is distinctive in this anthology is the way in which the poets have allowed the dybbuk to speak both through them in terms of history, tradition and memory , and for them in dealing creatively with this long shadow of the past. In so doing, an uneasy tension has been set up between a sense of the past and a living in the present. The drive to live in the present and yet to be rooted as Jewish women creates a dichotomy that cannot be resolved. Ironically it is in our struggle between surrender and flight from this confining shadow that we find what it is to be human.

Sonja Lyndon

Sylvia Paskin

We would like to dedicate this book with love to our daughters Nina and Zoe, our sons, Daniel, David and Leo, our mothers, Lilo and Mimi, and to our brothers, both named Peter, as well as to Paul and Tony who have been remarkable friends to both of us.

Sigrid Agocsi

APHORISM

I felt myself strange
in the country I grew up in.

Now having become a foreigner,
I have arrived at home.

HOMMAGE A ANNETTE VON DROSTE-HÜLSHOFF

Darkness. Slowly
sense after sense
is awakening -

Pictures are rising
from a long hidden
world.

And words suddenly
are finding their
way to it:

They are painting
the poem.

Liane Aukin

THE JEWISH FEMINIST WOMAN

Being a woman means
you have breasts,
a clitoris,
a vagina,
a womb
at least when you're born.
It means
you have menstrual periods
boys chat you up
you want to be attractive
you are expected to have children
to look after your parents
to be motherly.
It means
people depend on you
you're a good friend
men will tell you their innermost thoughts
you will inspire them.
It means you give more energy to creating an artist than
to being one.
It means
self sacrifice
it means, giving
it means self pity, regret, bitterness, resignation
it means
as you grow older, you come to terms with things.

Being a jewish woman means
they call you a princess
even though your father was poor and your mother dressed
badly.

It means the terrible history of your forebears.
It means
you're the sister, daughter, wife and mother
of men who are oppressed
it means
rabbis
whose wives wore wigs, their hair was shaved.
It means
you're self conscious when you eat a prawn
about your grandma's foreign accent
the fact you don't cook well
you worry about
marrying out of faith
will your child be called "dirty jew"
about not getting married.

It means
not knowing your lineage
or where your grandparents are buried
the original spelling of your name
whether your friends are anti-semites
does the school have a quota system
if it does - so? It's their right.

Being a jewish feminist means
you feel oppressed
by non-jews
By jews
by blacks - even.
It means resenting Zionism because
It produces a conflict of loyalties
about your country
your race
your sense of yourself
your wish to survive
to be identified
as an individual and as a member of the group.

It means
you question jewish history as written by men
by Josephus
by chassids
by Koestler.
You learn that
jewish women converted to Christianity for money in order
that
their husbands could continue to study the talmud
that their children could grow up well-fed
that their children should grow up.
It means
hating having to cook
trying to relate to non-jewish women and nearly succeeding.
It means
deciding whether or not your son is circumcised
should go to Israel.
It means
having nothing to do with your family
feeling guilty because your family are jewish
and proud
have suffered
have been gassed.
It means
knowing your father wanted you to
marry well
integrate
remain jewish
have upward mobility
care about your roots
never forget.
It means never wanting to step inside a synagogue
and when you do
feeling tenderness and loss and then
remembering
the women sat upstairs.
It means separating out national and racial cultures.

It means
like all women, having no country
unlike other jews
no homeland
no jewish feminist has visualised the promised land.
You remember
Golda Meir looked like Lyndon Johnson
that people think maybe Mozart was a jew
that
Rosa Luxemburg
Eleanor Marx
Emma Goldman
were jews and no-one mentions that.
It means
you are the mother, the daughter the sister the wife
of the chosen race
that you had no choice
it means
being Portnoy's complaint
and Freud's life work
and recognising the fact that
you're stuck with being jewish
so you might as well
try and define it.
But remembering
bagels and cheese
are a ball and chain
and my sister in Morocco
has never heard of kvetches.

HAIKU

Every deed
A footprint
In the snow
When spring comes

Joan Ballin

"VIENNA, SWEET CITY OF DREAMS"

Tea at three
A soft tinkling of
Silver forks
A sedate ritual of
Pouring and stirring
A quiet hum of
A Proper people
"Sachertorte bitte"

An exquisite slicing of
Thin black icing
A careful lifting
To thoughtful mouth
A slimy oozing
Of foul green liquid
As ashes fall
From my lips

Wanda Barford

FAMILY SNAPS

Here's one of grandfather's garden in Rhodes;
seven of us are in the group,
smiling the forced smile of photographs.

We're in two tiers with little me in front
eager to run off but restrained by a big hand.
My brother has put on his Colossus pose;
an aunt flicks forward two favourite curls.

Our oily skins tell of heat;
in the air orange-blossom and oleander...
not even the mulberries crushed blood-red underfoot
foretell anything but sweet air and everyday sorrows.

But another summer, much like this one,
the people of this garden (and it could have been me)
were pushed into boats and sailed to Piraeus;
then overland by cattletruck to Auschwitz.

My grandfather never got there.
For defying his SS guard
he was kicked to death on the train.

Granny, survivors said, went into the gas-chamber
carrying her soap and towel - she thought it was
a kind of Turkish bath like the one she used to visit

each Friday; I went with her
and when we came back home
it would be time to light the candles.

BEETROOT

Often, peeling beetroot, I think of you
my old young cousins, and I see your sunken eyes
and those numbers tattooed deep
into your fleshless arms.

Looking down at my stained fingers
I see your rouged cheeks faking health,
turned up to the guards, to plead
they postpone death a while.

The ruse worked for you; but for others
whose cheeks you painted - drained mothers
with pale children - it failed. They shuffled
into the gas chambers wearing this loud disguise.

SKY

*(to my mother Sarah Simson, born Rhodes 1903,
died Paris 1994)*

You would have loved the sky the day we buried you,
Of deep then deeper blue like on your island home,
The thinning poplars, planes shedding their mustard leaves.

There were no flowers — you hated cutting them —
But from your long-lost home a piece of rue
Thrown on the coffin lid beside your name.

The rabbi too the sort you would have liked: modest
In manner, crumpled suit, scuffed shoes, intoned the prayer
Basso profundo, with no sense of hurried time.

A few wore black, others, vivid colours; and some
Sobbed quietly, but no ululation or despair.
All round acceptance in that clear and weightless air

Of things that are and were and pass beyond
The limits of our bounded life. I heard your voice
Say: leave me now, I'm perfectly at peace.

And still I come to tell you this...you hated
Funerals, never spoke of them nor went to any.

ROMANY RHYME

Romany, Romany,
Where do you roam?
I've been down to Auschwitz
To visit my tomb.

Romany, Romany,
What did you there?
I saw a gold tooth
And a piece of black hair.

*500,000 Sinti and Romany gypsies were exterminated
in the concentration camps of the Third Reich.*

PRACTICALITIES
[A Found Poem]

The crematorium chief at Majdanek
had his own bathroom beside the ovens:
it was hot dusty work in the low-roofed,
iron-clad crematoria. The hours were long.

At Treblinka prisoners were made to do
exercises when they got off the train
to improve the circulation: carbon
monoxide takes effect more quickly then.

The furnace at Birkenau was supplied
by TOPF UND SÖHNE: the side door by THEO-
DOR KLEIN of Ludwigshafen. The maker's
stamp embossed on the side of the oven.

Block 10, Auschwitz the Racial Hygiene block;
stubby silver syringes inject phe-
nol straight into the heart. Death guaranteed
in two minutes and twenty seconds flat.

ALEX ZINK paid fifty pfennigs to buy
one kilo of human hair and turned it
into cloth; others stuffed mattresses. Gold
from fillings was taken to the Reichsbank.

AUT of Berlin supplied a two-furnace
crematorium, then a five-furnace one
to 'cope'. It cut incineration time
from one hour to nearly fifteen minutes.

When the crematoria could no longer
cope, great pyres were built fed by the fat of
burning bodies. Nothing must be wasted.
Extra fat was used for soap and candles.

The Zyklon B (hydrogen cyanide 'dis-
infector') was supplied to Auschwitz by
DEGESCH — twenty tons between '42
and '43; kitchens by HILDESHEIM.

Human compost endures.
Each winter in the forests
around Treblinka
fragments of bone
wash to the surface.
There's a mountain too
of artificial limbs,
a pretty wooden hand
with the nails etched
and painted pink
on the finger-tips.

And the suitcases
carrying the clothes
they would find again
'afterwards'
bear the owner's name
neatly inscribed:
'Else Meier, Köln'
'Simon Rosenberg, Berlin'
'Greta Schwartz, Hollandstraße, Wien'
'Lotte Rapaport, München'
'Norbert und Sigmund Steifel, Frankfurt'.

Janet Berenson-Perkins

THE CATERPILLAR

for S.

She lies inert, afraid to think,
cocooned in a duvet of lies.
Self-doubt, too heavy, suffocates;
her shaking hand cannot lift the weight,
paralysed by fear of her true nature.

Burning, drowning, choking on the pain,
she cannot see or feel her beauty.
A chrysalis in agony does not know
it is beginning its own metamorphosis.

THE ETERNAL LIGHT

Where does the past end?
I had a Jewish childhood -
Is it finished now?

Why then do the smells and sounds remain
so vibrant, echoing, sweet on my tongue?

Chicken soup, enshrined like madeleine,
evokes a steamy family babble.
Cross-current conversation
Everyone shouting,
Yet we all heard every word.

There was no rule book,
But we all knew the rules -
Golden ones and baser stuff.

Now floating in the sunlit Shabbos air
threads of prayer-songs rise from hibernation,
lace-winged by imperfect memory,
The tunes emerge, unsought, unthought.
The rising falling notes form faces -
Francine, Jerry, Mitch, Helene:
Where and who are they now?

Hayah, hoveh, yihyeh
L'olam va'ed

The Jewish spark cannot go out.

THE BOOK OF LIFE

So another chapter opens.
A leaf crackles as it's turned,
like dry paper skin.
Grandmother's face looks down
smiling her acceptance.
She doesn't need to know
how the story ends.
It's clear that she's been there.

The final chapter's written, read,
yet still unlived.

Can living change the words,
or are they the ink-stained path
that must be followed?

Where do we go from here?
Don't ask, just go there.
Turn the page.

Julie Bernstein

JUICE

What I was feeling
may not have been
lush, pink and mango-y,
but it was a crateful
of nectarines at least,
and now you've
shut the shop.
You said what you
were feeling was as
near to mango, passion
and guava as you
could get, and
I pictured an
exotic fruit future,
then you wanted
to 'move on', and
it was squashed.

RECLAIMING THE NIGHT

The dead girl walked
how she thought looked
confidently, into town
past the last people
to see her alive.
Would they remember
purple anorak,
green jeans,
shoulder-length brown hair?
Would they contact police
when 'Crimewatch' asked:
five feet small,
23 year-old woman,
final steps,
Thursday evening in May?

The reconstruction ran
her head through.
She stared hard
at passers by.
You will remember me.
I will be remembered.
Next time out
I'll wear something
outrageous.
A note was found:
"If I'm dead before 85
it wasn't my choice."
Death will be the one thing
I don't do quietly.

Nadine Brummer

HOUSE-GHOSTS

My richest aunt,
a house-a-holic, filled shelves and tabletops
with Toby jugs, cut glass and sundry silver cups.

She wanted life;
glass animals with scarlet eyes
winked in the lounge, cold cherries

teased overwrought
shepherdesses, and other porcelain toys
arched over by dimpled white erotic boys.

She colour-schemed,
lustily dressed windows, walls and floors
like a big brass band asking for applause.

My fastidious uncle,
thin as a magpie's tail, had a regimen
of easily digested food, low albumen,

but egg-custards nightly.
She, hugely fat, fed from filigree trays,
full of licorice allsorts on Sundays,

when family came,
a list of sisters, brothers, nephews, nieces,
in a part exchange of pecky kisses.

The front room babbled
clothes, recipes, a crescendo
of gossip which kept the whole show

on the road
since no-one need ever hear
another tell real anger, sorrow, fear.

In the other room,
cleverly apart, the uncles would dissect
the *Soviet Weekly* and the Rabbi's text.

And I at the edge
of two chattering crowds thought emptiness
blew up inside like bright Venetian glass.

Childless also
I still wonder if those baubles
worked for her, those gawish, lamentable

things; I try words
to lodge her lost ornaments,
house-ghosts all to whom I act as aunt.

OCCASION

There was this occasion
the days of the week worked up to
every seventh day. On the eve of the sabbath
my father, transformed by tallith
into someone more visibly dignified
than usual, held up a goblet
full of wine. He glittered like salt.

My mother clothed the table
in immaculate white, her hands
fluttered like trapped birds.
Three times she'd send forth
her hands to bring back hope,
returning they brooded over her eyes.
She lit the candles for the sabbath bride.

Two ascending flames brought
to an ordinary dark house
the candour of the sun, the moon's
illusions. Rage stood still;
quarrelling voices respectfully
changed language until
the candles guttered down, wax wept,
the acrid smoke of burned-out wicks
choked back our unspoken
'But we are entitled to be happy'.

Expectancy hung over our house
like fog the sun occasionally cracks.
That sabbath thing, the glimpse of
somewhere else, my father in voluptuous
white silk, my mother shielding her eyes
from the small furnaces fired
by an ordinarily struck match,
the sea-dark Alicante wine tasting
of waiting – there was this occasion
always about to happen.
It won't go out of my life.

LEAVING JERUSALEM

There were horns for sale,
rams' horns for remembrance,
and a neat man in a skull-cap who
brought out a bow of furrowed bone
and blew, ter-oo-ah,
as if his shop were Jericho,
as if those fractured calls
were quite an ordinary affair,
like sackbuts for dollars.

There were boxes full,
tusks, shafts, cusps,
dull white from Ashkelon,
and some the size of buffalo
black from Gilboa.

One, small enough to tuck into a pocket
would not have been dear,
and yet I could not bring myself to buy
the kind of voice you now hang on a wall,
just to retrieve childhood, Yom Kippur,
the congregation dumbstruck when
the cantor in his black plush hat
pursed his mouth. That bone-hard lip
and breath, perfectly controlled
showed how an animal might cry,
caught in a thicket.

AT THE LUCIAN FREUD EXHIBITION

Heads, hands, genitals and feet
are main events - he does them well.
Excess between is fleshed like meat.

And even now it takes some nerve to look
at turkey gizzards limp between men's legs
and women opening to a swarm of black.

Oh there's a buzz all right. Once at another show
I heard a woman in a hat enthuse
about a clever orchid, how

lips form a helipad for flies
which land in ruts, are trapped then sucked
where male and female parts are fused,

though none are needed for the helleborine
quite self-sufficient with its seed.
Can flowers be both gorgeous and obscene?

Leigh Bowery's back is overgrown with flecks,
an orchidaceous pink, buttocks sag
into an off-white stool. You sense the cracks

of old enamel bowls and chipped chrome taps
behind a drape. In front a red-brown rug
bristles. These genteel props

touch my eyes. Below each covering a frame,
upholding surfaces of this and that,
lies coiled, and I am forced to look again

at how I live. This cold October day
I'm in a crowd well-heeled and buttoned up
engrossed with such carnality

I fear our coats might flake and tear
and eyes, preoccupied with doubt,
find bodies we'd not bargained for.

SPOKE

Moving away how can you not miss
ceremony? Pesach, the door flung open
with the cry *'Baruch Haboh'*,

the irretrievable skill of the eye
glimpsing the wine go down in its silver cup,
your father's hand upholding.

Re-invent him now waiting for wings
to stream across his ordinary door-step,
reaching for tippet of angel or prophet.

And how can you not miss her
at the hiatus of a silence like oak,
expecting the silver axle-tree

to cleave the air brilliantly, like fire,
and, later, polishing a silver candlestick,
like a spoke wrenched from a perfect wheel.

Liz Cashdan

65+

Today, having the colour put back in my hair,
I read a brochure about the magic of Cornwall
derelict tin mines, reconstructed heritage,
and will I please fill in a questionnaire,
with a chance to win a holiday for two.
I hate having to tick the single box
(including widowed, separated and divorced)
but worst of all is the tick for age.

My pencil stays poised, won't make the mark.
Somewhere behind me in the scented heat
a radio voice tells of two old women
who left their sheltered homes, attacked
each other viciously, their joint ages
over one hundred and sixty years. Tick
too old for passion, too old for anger.

Well, you didn't still love me
when I was sixty-four
and now I'm past that,
into the last box
in the questionnaire.

I thought all those years ago
(in the forty-five plus box)
when the kids sang time away
on those French holidays -
tree-lined avenues in a yellow
submarine, in the diamond sky
with Lucy - I thought
Valentine, wine, need and feed
I've stated my point of view,
given my answer, mine for evermore.
Course I'll still love you
when you're sixty-four.

LUDWIKA CHOPIN; HER BROTHER'S LIFE

At home in Warsaw she is sorting his letters
remembers how in Paris they drank chocolate
she embroidered a slipper, copied pictures:
he found her tiny pencil on his piano.

He cannot remember the number of her house
every time he asks her anew.
He sends her books, music, a berceuse,
a mazurka for her little Ludwika.

A letter from Scotland where he is adored
and plays in all the big houses.
But Sunday, he says, no post, no railway,
no carriage, not even for a drive,
no boat
not even a dog to whistle to.

In London he is sick.
The English language is full of fogs and soot.
He dreams of Madame Sand in another country.

Back in Paris with the English fog lodged
in his throat and chest, he asks Ludwika to visit,
to bring her thimbles and knitting needles.
But she has no money for travel.

She finds his last pencilled note:
he is choking on his cough,
fears he may be buried alive.

Norma Cohen

LOVE IS A FLOWING PEN

Love is a flowing pen
that writes new promises
when limbs are open
and yield like dancers
to another's charms.
Lust attacks each moment
like tearing fruit
cartwheels through space
a warm wet belly without an ending
something to swim in,
float like a baby
not drown.

Sex without love
is a plunge into darkness
the flower opens briefly
to reveal its core
shyly
expectantly
till in a heart thud
flooded
it recoils
to suck its own sweetness

Sex without love
is an empty glass
there is no reflection
only a shudder of compressed passion
struggling to free itself
from the heat of the moment
Its warmth lingers only in a flicker
glints of rough diamond
and coils carelessly into sleep
like a lamp snuffed out.

I have a memory of another time
when the air hung sweet and light
time slurred between its clocks
laughter emptied without trying
an easy physicality
when I was young and shining
We marvelled at our newness
the pleasure in each other's smile
the eyes behind the door
the room clouded with light
you were full of grace
and in your eyes
I was gracious too
every step, every flutter, every word was right
and bounced back refreshed like a child.

Time hung
yes time hung for us alone
in charmed moments
I lit up, incandescent
mother lover child in play
sweet kisses tremble on the night sky
racing into passion
a passion not of lust but love
a passion of compassion
passion of frailty
where uncertainty turns into strength
I was solid then
fired by your admiration
your certainty of my existence

So why now, another time
am I gauche?
My feet slide away
I stutter helpless
in this sea of shifting frames
I stand waiting to be seen
craving the warm eyes of another day
to stretch me to my full height.
I am tied in leather cords
inarticulate trapped silent
blanked by fast streaming sentences
of another language
excluded by an alien badinage

I long to break free from this bondage
engage in a debate
to strengthen my muscle
a sinewy form of combat
a tug of war without handicaps
a more equal test of strength
to fire me into being
a chandelier
slowly spinning
unafraid
exultant
into the night
my body turning
in its own easy grace.

IF IF IF

If you fuck me over
I'll kill you
If you make a fool of me
I'll kill you
If you discount me
I'll scream so loud your blood'll curdle
and you won't be able to sleep
for the sound of eardrums
ringing passionately in the night
If you don't hear me screaming
I'll fight you and shout and shout and shout
until your head cracks startled against the wall
and my teeth will snap
violently with blood on the tongue
and my breath will rush out and freeze
in the air with nowhere to go
All the bones of my body will dissolve

all the skin of my body will char
slowly shrinking before your eyes
the eyes will glaze
the face will fall away
All the contours of a well known land will disappear
as the world slowly falls from a state of grace
the creases will uncrease
the mouth will unsmile
the eyes will unsee
the hands will unhold
the love will unlove
It's fire and flames and flashing knives
cacophony of spitting steel
revealing all things sharp and sensitive
a tremulous time
a dangerous time
Tread carefully my darling
beneath this frail skinned lover
lies an unknown thuggish landscape
urgent and bloody
in its hesitant delicate shell

Tricia Corob

NEPTUNE'S POOL

Glass stasis
of afternoon.
Surface
rarely creased by trees.
Ceaseless brilliance.

The fountain in Neptune's pool
dribbles slightly,
the reflection
unflinching.
Everything exists exactly
in two,
Scrolls of Medici iron
repeat;
lemons double,
a goldfish
carries another on its back.

Of course you're invisible.
You seem too much yourself
to split in two.
You would shatter the moveless centuries
out of this reflective shroud:

imagine Neptune's stone
abstracted and him striding over the water...
The lemon trees scream
the sedate florentine smile
breaks.

But you are invisible.
I peer into the pool:
my dark face
doubles.

EARTH COERCES

Earth coerces
sucks
her rhythm
into mine.

I'm drawn into fibres
and porousness.
A pulse compels my feet -
they root and twine

delve mauve bruising
for new violets.
My veins submit
to ignite the crocuses.

Earth ignores my whims.
Melts me, ekes me out
like wax. My dripping
feeds greeness.

I glide leaf-sheens
and daffodil lips
am lissom among grasses
stirred to the red

smart of breaking buds.

THE FUNICULAR

We were in a queue for the funicular.
Alps white and sheer on every side.
Geometry of fir trees.
We get jostled, pushed

suddenly you're about to get in
a glass case
hang in space
without me.

I push into the crowd,
shout 'We're together - we're together'
but I can't get through.
I remember ancient separations

being forced apart
gas chambers

then I see you beside me.
The funicular swings
harmlessly
in perfect blue.

Lynette Craig

EXILED

I shall see the lake in winter,
watch men spread nets under the ice,
I shall ride the sledge to fetch beans
and banter with a toothless old man
who holds the horses. I shall cut
wood from the forest to build our home,
I shall steal a taste of cherry wine
and pack my brother's clothes..

He can't stay,
too many questions -
he had to say his brother
was dead - the girls
growing - the wife, nag, nag -
surely the letter will come.
How he longs to walk paved streets, hear
sewing machines
clack out their welcome.

He talked of lakes,
my grandfather,
and forests on his father's land.

He loved the open fields -
fresh-laid eggs he charmed
from farmer's wives.
Silently he wept over letters
only he could read,
his children teased him
out of sadness
- they let it go -

IN THE PICASSO HOUSE, PARIS

in a hot flush of understanding
I know this woman - she is
dizzy from looking in two directions
her single-breasted terror
looks out at me
and I stare back

I TAKE THESE TABLETS

I take these tablets
like a prayer -
each night.

This is my prayer:
that someone in his lab
got it right, despite
terrible pay, no promotion
and a shrewish wife.

"A SAD TALE'S BEST FOR WINTER"

..and so the story in our family says
she married him, there in the market place
next to the stall her mother kept
- fish silent witnesses as the glass
cracked beneath his heel.
Leaves swirled around the canopy,
she bowed her head, her long brown hair
hung down across her face.
She told her mother she would visit soon
but wondered when.

The months went by and in the Spring
the handsome pair rode into town
in silk and fur with jewels about their necks.
She hugged her mother, kissed and laughed -
all was well, the match was sound,
she held her hand upon her waist
and blushed, her plaited hair revealed
her reddened cheeks.

He left her in the wooden house for days
deep in the forest, miles from any road -
she cleaned and cooked and sewed white
linen tablecloths; she welcomed him
when he returned each time with gifts
and questioned him about the world she missed.
The house was hers but for one room
which he had locked...

It was winter, a cold December night,
the baby sleeping, sucking at his thumb,
she noticed that the key was in the lock
of the forbidden room. In the icy gloom
she saw the piles of guns and gold.

All through the frozen forest
back to her mother's house, she rode,
howled out her sorrow to the cold moon and
locked the baby tight against her heart.

Years passed, the child grew strong
wise and comely by his mother's side.
They loaded fish onto the market stall
together, love smiled between them
until that day - she knew that it would come -
her husband walked across the square
and took her by the arm. All that they heard,
was "I will have the boy"...

WEAPONS - FOR - JEWS

Headline in The Independent 19.11.1990
It was alleged that the Israeli government traded weapons
for Ethiopian Jews

Am I worth a fragmentation bomb?
A shell or two, perhaps
a tank?
No, not a tank.

Measure me in flowers,
a field of rarest fritillaria,
heads bent to withstand
the unexpected gusts of early spring;
or that old rose
which clings onto the house
bride - blushing every June
year in, year out.

Count me in laughs,
belly - stretching blue -
Have you heard the one about....?

Sing me in old songs
like my father sang
to lull me into sleep:
Miss Otis' never - ending regrets
bought my innocent repose.

Free me, by all means,
I should like to leave..

Look at the colour photograph.
There beneath the blankets
the label says,
a small grenade.

Iona Doniach

WHY IS IT THAT SOME WOMEN

Why is it that some women still
carry the message that their mothers gave them
holding deep inside the negative

Why is it that some women walk free and proud
letting leaves and feathers
fall around their hair

And why is it that some women wear hats
and at every turn of their heads
stately and sure they smile
until the immediate word disappears
in a pool of light

Why is it that some women
cherish and hold another dear
and have the ability to walk the full length
of the upward path

And why is it that some women reach the end
to sit and wait staring at the sky
wearing the transparent cloth of sleep.

Jane Dorner

DON PASQUALE

On stage. The notary unrolls,
Swirls sealing-wax and ribbon
At his velvet ruffled cuffs.
Quill flourish, he pronounces
A mockery of conditions
That bind this man to that girl
And stamps the mime charade
With a dandy bow.

In the stalls. He squirms beside
His opera-coated wife
And wonders why she argues
When he bought her those pearls.
Snatching the roll of parchment
In his turmoiled mind
To ink it with his own demands,
Blotting where she failed him.

Outside. The crush doors open
To a corridor of concrete
Where sleeping-bagged lie
John and Maggie huddled together
Against the wind-toothed cold,
Bound only by the law
That lives and lets live –
With all the twangs on music's strings.

LINES TO THE WORD PROCESSOR

Teach me how to cut and paste
To edit out the parts that are not neat
Retrieving a clean crisp laser print
From the wrinkled scrawl of a sullied sheet

Teach me how to search and replace
The sour taste of inelegant lines
To repaginate and undo
Find better words for other times

Teach me how to define styles
To weave a text with untangled strands
Keeping the headings separate
And the paragraphs in different bands

Teach me how to open and to save
Playing with thoughts unattached
Fingering with point and click
Mutely pressing for the trick
To close files that are not matched
And find the self that has been snatched

Ruth Fainlight

DINAH (GENESIS 34)

"High-spirited and martial men among all nations and
throughout history have often yielded to blind cruelty when
dealing with an outrage of this nature."
(note to Genesis 34:31, Soncino Pentateuch & Haftorahs)

Holding up my hands in warning,
I want to call, "No! No! Don't do it!",
to Shechem and Dinah, to Simeon and Levi,
but most of all, to every able-bodied male
of Hamor's tribe. "Don't consent, it's a trap."

Swollen tender flesh:
Shechem's, aching with lust and love
(he told his father, "Get me this damsel to wife",
he "spoke comfortingly unto the damsel");
Dinah's broken maidenhead;
Hamor's guards, weakened by pain,
three days after circumcision.

That was the moment chosen to destroy them,
spoil the city, take their flocks and herds,
enslave their wives and little ones, while
Dinah's brothers led her back to Jacob's tents,
ancient honour satisfied.

Jacob chided his sons, fearful
that Canaanites and Perizzites
would now combine against him.
Not until he lay dying
did he curse them for that wild vengeance.
Whether Dinah was saddened by
Shechem's death is never mentioned.

"No, no, don't do it!",
I want to call out,
palms upward, heart pounding.
"Choose another future!"
But it's always too late or too soon.
So much still must happen.
The story has only started.

LINEAGE

When my eyes were sore or tired or itched,
clenching her hand in a loose fist,
my mother would rub her wedding ring,
carefully, along the closed lids,
sure the touch of gold was curative.

She also believed in hot water
with lemon, first thing in the morning
and, at any time of day, drank awful-
tasting infusions and pot-liquors
to purify her blood. She warmed
a spoonful of sweet almond oil to pour
into my aching ear, wrapped torn
old woollen vests around my throat,
and blistered my chest with a poultice
if I came down with a cold.

59

Remedies and simples from the old
country, still useful in the city,
were passed from mother to daughter
and not yet scorned. We rarely saw
a doctor. When I was little
it seemed normal to be sickly
for half of the year. I never told her
that I was proud she was a witch.

Rachel Castell Farhi

SUITE TWO-THREE-SIX AT THE KING DAVID

Satin-shoed, white-veiled,
you carry me over the threshold of no.236; we laugh

Burst in upon the blue and green suite at midnight
and whatever spirits of former inhabitants might be there,
are exorcised by our laughter,
our new joy,
a talisman against the dark.

The bed! - a huge green and gold affair.
We laugh again - it's the first time we've had a decent bed to
love upon.

Childlike,
we throw ourselves upon it, test it out,
bouncing and giggling - a love trampoline -

Until I remember and look at you
And you look back at me
Remembering also.

We watch each other,
Animalesque,
with old-new eyes.
"Kalati," - my bride, you whisper
And our passion turns to shyness at our new selves.

A desert moon searches us out through the window
I can see the walls of the Old City in the distance
It's eye-gates witness our consummation.
The words of the *ketubah* are still fresh in our hearing;
We are a religious transaction - my ring a symbol of a 5000
year old bargain struck;
The marriage parchment my legal guarantee against you.

Already we feel the first link in the chain of tradition begin
to bind us.
Yesterday we were ourselves,
Tonight -
"Al dabri!" - don't speak! you say,
And the warmth of your lips against mine
Seals my silence.

IN REMEMBRANCE OF LOVERS PAST -
HOLOCAUST DAY

When they sounded the siren today
and time stood still,
I watched your blue eyes weaken,
And in their reflection I saw us,
You and I,
Lovers,
Jews,
And more than two thousand years behind us,
The ancient curse of an exiled People
Borne across our shoulders.

You and I were lovers from Creation
And through ages past,
Though our bodies were weakened and bruised,
Our hopes burned on in darkness.
We knew they could not be extinguished.

62

I knew the strength of your body,
Long before they took us from our Land and into bondage.

I knew the gentleness of your skin,
Long before the Inquisitor's iron brands.

I knew the look of anger in your eyes,
Long before they spat at us and burned our ghetto.

And I knew you loved me still,
Even as we were made to walk apart into the gas.

When they sounded the siren today,
My eyes flowed with tears I did not want to cry.
And in their bitter waters I saw us,
You and I,
Lovers,
Jews,
In the land of our redemption.

Elaine Feinstein

VALENTINE FOR A MIDDLE-AGED SPOUSE

Dear Love, since we might both be dead by now
through war, disease, hijack or accident
at least for one day, let's not speak of how
much we have bickered, botched and badly spent.
Wouldn't it make much more sense to collude
in an affectionate work of camouflage,
turning our eyes away from all we've skewed,
to the small gains of household bricolage?
As our teeth loosen and our faces crag
(I shall grow skinnier as you grow paunched,
a Laurel to your Hardy, not much brag),
I'll think of all our love most sweetly launched
if you look with favour on these lines
we may live as tender valentines.

MOTHER LOVE

You eat me, your
nights eat me.
Once you took
haemoglobin and bone
out of my blood,

now my head
sleeps forward on my neck
holding you.

In the morning my
skin shines hot
and you are happy
banging your fat hands.

I kiss your
soft feet mindless:
delicately

your shit slides out
yellow and
smelling of curd cheese.

ROSE

Your pantry stocked with sweet cooked fish,
pink herring, Polish cucumbers
in newspaper, and on the gas
a bristly hen still boiling into soup:
most gentle sloven, how I honour now
all your enormous, unfastidious welcome.

And when the string of two brown carrier bags
bit into your short fat fingers
you only muttered, doesn't matter. I didn't understand
why you continued living with a man
who could not forgive you, could not

forgive your worst offence:
your happiness in little.
Even a string of shells would give you pleasure,
but we did not bring gifts often;
and now it is too late to thank you for
the warmth of your wide bosom, and the dimpled arms
waiting to hug my own bewildered children.

AGAINST WINTER

His kiss a bristling
beard in my ear, at 83:
"aren't you afraid of
dying?" I asked him (on his knee).
who shall excell   his shrug for answer?

and yet was it long after,
senile, he lived in our front room,
once I had to
hold a potty out for him, his
penis was pink and clean as a child

and what he remembered of
Odessa and the Europe he walked through
was gone like the language I
never learned to speak, that
gave him resistance,

and his own sense of
favour   (failed
rabbi, carpenter,
farmer in
Montreal)

and now I think
how the smell of
peppermint in his yellow
handkerchieves and the
snuff marks under his nose

were another part of it:
his sloven grace
(stronger than abstinence) that
was the source of his
undisciplined stamina.

Thilde Fox

YOM KIPPUR

We were hungry often enough
he said to her clutching
his plate as if he would
send it back to his
aching self. At once
the claws of hunger pounced out
from the stretched nerves
of his memory and scraped
at his paunch and tore
at his dry throat the forest
closed over him
he picked up a morsel
and pushed it into her mouth.

INHERITANCE

I gave you a new world, where yellow stars
light children's books, trains go on holiday,
and when you raise your face into the shower,
and hold the pink soap, you remember only
the nice boy waiting in your soft clean bed.
You sing their music and move to their speech.

One other gift I gave unwillingly.
You look Jewish.

Berta Freistadt

TOYS FOR PHARAOH

for Primo Levi's wife

This time
The women took
Toys and cushions
The mothers
Just as then it was
Timbrels and drums
Happily
The children
Were mostly dead
Before they wore out
You know how they
Won't share and squabble
And whine when things break

It was hate
That kept us going
This time
Those who did
Not flight
You had music and blisters
The fear of a knife in the back
Salt water washing your heels
To keep you alive
We had the numbers
The left and the right
The drowning shame
Of unwashed consciences
The daily presence of death

If only we had had music
There was the need
To kill the sound of our thoughts
For the beauty
The tap to pain
You could have had the cushions
To soften the icy sand
Given the toys to Pharaoh
He had children

WE SEE HER

We see her
Everybody's aunt
The wife, the Jewish
Mother
We know her familiar bulk
Covered, respectable
The bright shine of
Finger waves above
Tired floury cheeks
We smell her
She is noodle and strudel

We see her
By a wall stopped
'Die Juden'
Fumbles in a bag
Dark
Capacious as experience
Is it a handkerchief
In her hand
To mop wet memories
Or something else?
She turns
A small smile on her lips
We read *'Die Juden*
Sind Wunderschön'

The bag clasp clicks
She moves on
Keeping her eyes
Skinned

SHAME

Sitting in the singing
Drenched in song and shame
Finger chasing glyphs
Eye on the english
Heart on god
Over people's shoulders
I shape-watch for the place
Follow prayers by outline
Blessings by the printed length

All around mouths move
Only mine is still
They wash over me the words
Hypnotic sensual
Each vowel joins each woman
Lip to lip stronger than kissing
I sway beat my feet
See how I join in
When I know the tune
I hum
Yet my lips are motionless
Humming is drowned
Useless
Quick I grab the few phrases
That have sunk in
Pidjin on the back of melody
It washes over me shame
Nauseous burning

Drowning again
In words that are noise
Stranger in my own house
Strange tongue resounding
I submit at last to loss
Stop trying
Too tired for all this deciphering
Too tired to push
This rock. To swim.

Adèle Geras

COMPOSER

She is chopping onions, listening to Mozart's *Requiem*,
She imagines the kitchen ceiling vaulted and gilded,
ornately scrolled, thronged with angels.

Her knitted shawl on the table,
(magenta, turquoise, silver, blue and black, randomly
striped)
is nothing but a soft place for her sleeping cat
who knows everything about harmony,
and can recognise a pleasing contrast
with her dark tiger-markings
when she sees one.

THE CURATOR

Every photograph
and paper is important.
The glass preserves them.

The visitors come
looking for what they have lost
and for who they were.

I point out faces,
decipher the faded names,
stroke the ancient maps.

My nights are filled with
flat phantoms in black and white
and the smell of ash.

Every new morning
I must look at them again
and speak for them all.

BETWEEN THE LINES

Dovercourt. December 1938

Mama darling everything is fine.
(where are you   where is your smell   when you kiss me)

Everyone is being very kind.
(but sometimes i do not know what they are saying
we see a lot of teeth   i think they are smiling
but he smiled too mama do you remember
just as though the blossoming of glass
into galaxies of diamonds was better than music   he smiled
to hear his own black fist exploding through the mirror
and how can what he did not bring bad luck)

There is a chocolate here called Mars
(and they have puddings like cold sweet vomit
lumpy and almost white   over and over i say
coffee cinnamon kuchen strudel to see
if the words will help   coffee cinnamon
kuchen strudel)

and a brown drink tasting of salty meat.
We are near the sea,
(cold who would have thought it could be so cold
and where does skygrey end and seagrey start   i miss
big buildings shops pavements lines
and lines of streetlights parks and bandstands silly
trumpetty oompah songs   also you mama and papa
all the annoying relatives   my soft bed   angelika my doll
who would have filled my suitcase   oh mama please
look after her   take her out of the toy cupboard
and kiss her for me please   i miss my life   that's
what i miss   more than anything)

We can see it from the windows.
Everyone is being very kind.
England is lovely. Please come soon.

Miriam Halahmy

MAKING KUBEH

She sits in my kitchen making kubeh
the ancient way
with her hands.
She always cooks with her hands.

She pats the moist semolina in her palm
fashioning little cakes.
Pushing in tiny meatballs
she seals the edge with finger and thumb.
Flesh
swelled with age
squeezes the single gold band.
Chipped red nail varnish
gaily belies the olive skin
wrinkled again and again like the desert floor.

My small son
eager to shape the dough in his hand
reaches out.
His flesh
chubby with youth
brushes against her fingers
peacefully working the day.

Between their touch lies the moment of learning
                                    of passing on
                                    of generation.

The grandmother and the child
making kubeh in my kitchen
the ancient way.

EULOGY

(for my mother)

She is a crocus bulb
cradled in earth
nose pointed to spring.

She is a grass blade
green, knifesharp
breath frozen in wind.

She is warm scent of oven
soft skin
a cardigan, pink and black stripe.

She is a watch, 2 am
final heartbeat
yahrzeit candle in the night.

WASHING APPLES

Like Mandela casting his vote, I smile
and peel Cape stickers from green apples,
reel back years of vigil, marches,
taking my small son to sign.

He knows now why I said
at street stalls, in supermarkets, not those, or those
why it was never just an apple.

HUNTING SHELLS BY THE SEA OF GALILEE

(May 1988)

I
The flowers of the jacaranda trees are falling
end of May.
She runs ahead scooping pale lilac.
Beyond the hotel hills open up
the vast blue sea.
Wild cats, scavenger thin,
skulk behind boulders.
I take her hand to watch the evening light.

II
Across the Galil in lemon groves
hillsides thick with olive,
intifada
anger rooted as the swaying palm
ignites the honeyed land.
Soldiers, humiliated but not beaten,
point guns, swear they never fire.
Rocks fall like rotten manna
on broken promises, shattered sunlight.
Newspapers reek of torture, prison fever.
We avoid Jerusalem,
fear stalks our route map south.

77

Joyce Herbert

INTERROGATION OF A LITTLE GIRL IN THRACE

(a photo of this child is in The Holocaust by Martin Gilbert.)

You stood up straight
in front of the table,
politely waiting your turn.

Strong in the sun,
you spoke for yourself.

Child of the dark,
you had played all the time there was,
and you were sent in a sealed box car
from the place where your warmth had been.

FOR MARC CHAGALL

The bride with a fan is a dream, she
flies about the paintings
in the colours of dusk,
or singing in red,
crouched asleep or vibrating,
running back with your flowers.

She's a leaping fish,
a cow with soft eyes,
the warmth in a wooden house
you carried in your head.

She's young, moist in her sap,
holding you among violins and prophets
where no hands can reach,
and you've gone back
across the rooftops
to the four walls of love.

JEWISH CEMETERY, MERTHYR

They grow from the mountain,
tall, stubborn, the Hebrew
lacing them.

Sunk long ago
with love and weeping,
left in this groove of the hills.

They mark where prayers
fell like rain:
stand in eroding winds,
listen for young voices.

Nini Herman

YOU GAUNT GREY FIGURE...

You gaunt, grey figure of a Russian writer,
Who haunts my lonely nights, long before dawn,
This darkest of the winters of my lifetime,
The bitterest that I have ever known.

There falls a day in every lifetime,
There is no-one outside the door,
Its locks and bolts need never be unfastened,
With eager haste that drew them back, before.

When no more footsteps cross the empty garden,
To spoil the cold perfection of the snow,
When nothing moves among the deadly tree trunks,
And makes the listlessly suspended hour glow.

And yet, and yet with courage at its lowest,
The ticking of the heart so faint and slow,
Appears the famous consolation
Intended for the need to know.

There is no man can fill his stature,
Nor soul at random be induced to grow,
Till measured against cataclysms,
That man might wish no man to know,

And looking back across the anguished ages,
That we would banish, if we but knew how,
Seeing a flimsy candle burning
At every place where someone's hopes lay down,

The darkness opens like a door and leaves me
A long procession winding dimly through the night,
So merged and muffled that it might escape me
But that its length and breadth is measured out in light.

And yes, I know now, why you visit,
The unwound hours in this silent home,
Just to confirm this is as you found it,
When you had almost thought you were alone.

I THINK THE FIELDS WILL GREEN AGAIN

I think the fields will green again
I think the corn will rise,
And empty nests be home again,
And things half dead, alive.

I heard a little broken pot
Click whole again and sing,
O, no-one owed me anything,
And least of all a spring.

Tamar Hodes

VIRGINIA

There were too many deaths.

Strands of hair fell from the tight bun
madness dying beneath the smile.

She could write, rewrite
streams and clouds of it.
The vision tunnels blind
and stumbles upon meaning.
Circling under the tides of London
life refreshes those who choose to drink.

Bloomsbury spun.
What gives birth gives death.
The laughing choke on salmon bones
return to water. Drown.

But she was the queen
eating impulse and washing in it.
A wild chase for detail.
Put the butterfly under the microscope.
Look, and sadly, be cruel to look.

LANGUAGE

"When autoclaved, panel changes from pink to dark brown."
Dressing wrapper
Regional Sterile Supply Unit
West Midlands Regional Health Authority

"...and there'll be some rather untidy weather today."
Rob McElwee
Radio 3, Thursday 13 May, 1993

While cleaning the loo and recalling
90% of dust is dead skin
and one can define the lowest of the house by she who
cleans the loo
I hear the weather forecast
then read the dressing wrapper.

Having wondered what to write about
and feeling uninspired by the poppies in the garden
(however bright)
and the blue sky
(however textured)
I am thrown into searching about me
and concluding that poetry is there,
has always been there,
on the tongues of suited weathermen
and formed by the moist lips of market traders
as their words disappear in the air.

I snatch
words from everywhere.

SOME FLY, SOME SETTLE

Flies his kite, the old man
on Parliament Hill.
Red bows. A string of freedom.

                                                    The lily opens

I do not love you, she whispered
coffee burning the pot.

                                                    White

Paper on pavements.

                                                    Blown

Heron floods clouds.
The kite, the old man,
Parliament Hill.

                                                    Still

Skies close.
Men on dirty trains.
The drawing of blinds.

                                                    The lily closes

Kites fold.
Dead moths are brushed from window sills.

                                                    The lily locks

THE PAGE TURNER

I knew it was dangerous to trust my wife
but she's turned pages for me all my life.

That's the way I liked it -

me, the star, in control,

(and at a nod of my statuesque head)

she turned, just one

single

page at a time.

But that night

in the slow movement of Shostakovitch's second,
(you know, in F, my party piece)

we reached the penultimate page

last bar

last note

and she did not turn.

And my hands froze

and there was a silence
where there should have been music.

I have not forgiven her.
Now when she says, "Come for dinner,"
or "Come to bed"
or "Take me shopping"

I turn my head and pretend I have not heard her.

Sue Hubbard

ASSIMILATION

I never knew whether to say Amen.
In the vaulted hall silent girls dipped
rosy profiles into dust freckled sunlight

while I stood dumb-lipped trapped by
the trinity of longing, fear, propriety,
the word still-born in my throat.

Alone at thirteen in shadows of Dresden
blue, I bore the guilt of history, somehow
felt the weight of censure for what they'd done.

Head bowed consulting the diamond perforations on
regulation shoes, burnt ashes branded my tongue
with the double stigmata: unbeliever, hypocrite.

I did not know where I'd come from but guessed
at their journey through the snow flecked storms
of some Lithuanian December night

creeping through purple larch and spruce to flee
the zealous pogroms and their indignant Slavic rage.
Yet I've never tasted the sweet wine of Kiddush.

Beyond the stained glass windows and the Annunciation
English playing fields stretched printed with
tramlines, the watermarks of fair play.

In the back of the cupboard in my father's study
a tarnished silver samovar lay in waiting for
tall glasses, lemon and a scoop of Russian tea.

INHERITANCE

Childhood Sundays: the dread,
and the polished patina of oak
with crimson claret, the snowy
linen in initialled silver rings
and hexagrams of cutlery on
tablemats of hunting scenes -
pink coats and fox-hounds braying
for the kill and my father skilfully
carving the strained lacunae
thin as slices of rare beef.
Days when grandma came, the air
was sharp as English mustard
- she wouldn't eat the meat,
instead brought pots of pickled
cucumber, chopped liver, balls
of *gefilte* fish in waxy paper-bags
which made my mother sigh.
"It's not kosher" grandma said
when I asked <u>why?</u> unlocking
clouded memories, three generations'
climb from East End tenement
to this wooden Surrey Hill.
This was a house of tea cups,
of cupboards layered with mounds
of my father's crisp starched shirts,
of rose beds and clipped lawns,
where I learned to stitch on
that elastic tennis-club smile
to cover the slow dawning
that I was a Jew.

ROOMS

Out beyond the half-shadows
of silent rooms where dust
collects between the keys
of unplayed pianos, gathers
along hidden picture rails
and coats in a willow-pattern
bowl, greying cubes of sugar,

out beyond the lamp-light,
the yolked rim seeping
cinnamon rings onto Persian
rugs and the smeared glass,
past the crabbed cherry
the lavender and mint,
the barbs of rosemary
and pots of withered balm,

past the privet and the creosoted
fence where embers flicker
like bated breath among
piles of sodden leaves
and the smell of wood-smoke
rises in October air
catching the nostrils
like the memory of a memory,

beyond these there is only
something felt, something
inaudible, an impossible
longing rising in a plume
of wood-smoke beyond the hedge
and herb-garden, the lamp-light,
like dust settling between
the cracks of floor-boards,
coating the forgotten sugar.

WOMAN BATHING IN A STREAM

Some days Bathsheba or Danaë
voluptuous and bangled
on her cushioned ottoman. But this evening,
her linen chemise crumpled high
against wide hips, the loose
sleeves carelessly rolled, she paddles
the stream, simply herself, Hendrickye.

Florentine brocade, mulberry damask
from Uzbekistan, she leaves the tumbled rugs,
steps in the pool, her body warm, the smell
of him lingering still between her thighs.
His eyes absorb the creamy solid flesh,
those familiar dimpled knees. He makes
no judgement on her nakedness.

Times she has posed for him;
out of love, not an interest in his art,
just as each morning she pours his ale
chops pickled herrings, slices coarse black bread,
nights warmed his bed since Saskia died.*
Nurse to small Titus, what difference,
opening her ample arms to him as well.
No matter others find him strange.

Soon dusk will turn to night, wood smoke
and a Gouda moon hung over the gabled house.
She turns to the mirror, combs out her hair
prepares for sleep, sees other selves reflected
in her glass; the sandy freckled skin. Let him
wrap her in *chiaroscuro* if he must - grey morning
will find him seeking the warmth of her bed.

Saskia was Rembrandt's first wife, Titus his son

THE CURSE

She is all woman now
daughter become sister
spindle-prick of peony
smearing her whites.

A butterfly wing of bright
crimson surprises her waking,
shyly the comes to me bringing her
ring-o-roses, her scarlet bouquet.

We are joined in blood
by the slow pull of the moon's
waning and the small secrets
of darkened bathroom shelves.

How the past echoes. My mother's
silent mouthing of those witch-craft
words. The Curse, as she taught me
to name that first straining.

Have we forgotten those cackle
voices; conspiratorial whispers
echoing among unguents and tinctures
in white-tiled rooms?

And I who was mute, spineless
as a sea-horse, wish you brave
and beautiful. Feel your roots, deep
and damp, as rusty beets smelling of earth.

Judith Issroff

I SHALL MISS YOU MOTHER....

I am grateful for these quiet days,
this chance to be together - the natural state,
to try to come to terms with, to share with you awhile
your gentle yet oh so achey
fading away.

You may be close,
but I am not yet ready
for you to pass over
the edge of life....
but I don't want you to suffer.

I am grateful you are alive still
to the nuances of the days,
enjoy with me the unfolding of a leaf,
some human foible, music,
find whatever's out of place and needs attention,
are still eager to complete the crossword puzzle
or to beat me in Scrabble.

When your time comes
I hope you will go with grace.
It may not be but know that
I would prefer to be with you
holding your hand.
We both have endured
too great a measure of loneliness.

And just once, may your ticket or token win,
for your patience deserves it
and then I know you will go proudly
leaving more than merely the memories I will cherish
and your offspring,
though for me my life is really quite enough,
for which I thank you.

WE WILL LIVE QUIETLY

We will live quietly,
argue only about Zionism
and the dubious privilege of our Jewish birth
which so richly entitles us to a
compound, complex distillate
of the essence of human suffering
for a disintegrated tribal totem
and a great idea
which failed to save us or our ancestors from others, or from
ourselves -
we will read more books, write some,
cook, & keep somewhat casual house and hours.
we will go on listening to Mozart, Schubert, Chopin,
(& the Bs & the rest)
we will grow
fruit and vegetables,
flowers and poems,
and
our love
to whatever age we be granted this grace

and regret
only that we didn't start doing so sooner
despite
the inescapable undertow of our separate sadnesses.

will we?

WRITING, PAINTING,

just beginning and beginning,
trying
ways of discovering, growing... maybe...
going somewhere, not yet anywhere....
taking risks,
living,
marking time -
like Dali's weeping watches
making marks,
splotches of colour,
respecting Aboulafia[*], clearing the mind
to allow the letters/words through
a kind of purifying process,
working with turmoil and tumult
to a state of balanced energy and excitement
more or less communicable

[*] *The 14th Century mystic Jew fasted, prayed, then let G-d's
sacred letters flow through him shaping words to direct his
spirit to mount the five-stepped ladder of wisdom and
enlightenment to soul and G-d knowledge.*

SINAI

Tonight I am in London:
the sound of water splashing
and the moon, full, evoke
        the monastery terrace -
Santa Katerina in the hills:
        luminescent rockslopes, mountains forever
          ("new", you said, and told tales of Turks
            and monks building mosques)
You   ...   and men talking:
You   ...   (your leg must have been smashed in the
            war, or...I never asked)
        the cold stone on my bottom
          you didn't know was bare;
        that fishy smell;
        desert dogs howling
and the silence.....
        Bedouin men and camels moving,
merging into shadows, into ground;
        centuries of pilgrims;
        war and peace,
such peace   such heavy content...
        ("Don't change!" you said, "Stay different.
          Stay as you are!")
Morning stirred the sleepers:
        the camelmen squatted in the sand
          and prayed, or excreted, or both.
Astride 'my' camel, soothing, sensual under,
my eyes were free to drink the shapes of mountains
        moonlit, starlit, sun-tongued, sun-smeared,
          and seared
- the sun blinded -
as tonight, in London, this full moon.

Shirley Jaffe

LOOKING BACK OR AREN'T YOU GLAD YOU'RE NOT AN ELEPHANT

Looking for signs
Looking hopeful
Looking in at the doctor's
Looking for the post....
Looking delighted
Looking at names
Looking at Victoria and Victor.

Looking at books
Looking into the Leboyer Method,
Looking convinced
Looking at the Leboyer Clinic
Looking at the Bank Statements....
Looking for the National Childbirth Trust
Looking at Hospitals
Looking at Francoise - or Robert.

Looking peaky
Looking for the Rich Tea Biscuits
Looking fragile
Looking late for work
Looking green
Looking for somewhere to be sick....
Looking wretched
Looking for sympathy
Looking for anything I can bear to eat
Looking at Cassandra - or Ezekiel?

Looking a BIT better
Looking at the bump
Looking well
Looking at the bump moving
Looking at exercise classes
Looking for pickled cucumber
Looking up knitting patterns
Looking for Size 13 needles?
Looking for where I've dropped the stitch
Looking for Mu-um....
Looking at the family bible
Looking at Martha - or Joseph?.....

Looking fit
Looking for peanut butter sandwiches - AND pickled cucumber
Looking energetic
Looking for paper for the spare room
Looking at paint colours
Looking at Amber or Primrose - or Leonardo?
Looking at carrycots
Looking at prams....
Looking at bank statements....
Looking in Exchange and Mart
Looking for a "last fling"
Looking around Stratford-Upon-Avon
Looking at Juliet - or Benedict?

Looking good
Looking bonny
Looking fat
Looking gross
Looking for a diet with blackcurrent icecream - AND pickled
   cucumber
Looking for something to wear
Looking for ANYTHING to wear
Looking at what Sue lent me
Looking for anything I can get INTO
Looking at what Mum found in the attic from when she had
   ME
Looking pre-historic
Looking at Britannia - or Beowolf.

Looking at maternity allowances
Looking at the bank statement
Looking at commuting
Looking hot and tired
Looking at swollen ankles
Looking in on my midwife
Looking at my blood pressure....
Looking at my leaving presents
Looking relaxed
Looking for a chair to put my feet up
Looking relaxed;
Looking round my garden
Looking at Rose - or DAISY - OR - OR - YES, Robin!

Looking restless
Looking for the days to pass
Looking enormous
Looking colossal
Looking like a waddly hippopotamus....
Looking full of energy
Looking round the spare room
Looking at all the stuff that has to go somewhere else
Looking at the house I've just spring cleaned
Looking at the calendar
Looking at the clock....
Looking at the clock a contraction later
Looking at Jane Austen, but not reading
Looking at Emma - or Darcy

Looking for a taxi
Looking for my midwife
Looking apprehensive
Looking determined
Looking damp and exhausted
Looking at my husband rubbing my hands....
Looking for relief
Looking for gas and air
Looking at a room that seems filled with light
Looking for strength for just one more push
Looking for that last colossal effort.....

Looking amazed
Looking exultant
Looking at the bluest eyes I've ever seen
Looking full of love and contentment
Looking ..... at Imogen.

REFLECTION

I used to be young, and sometimes pretty,
But that was a while back; and oh!, it is hard
To see in the glass the unfamiliar, ageing woman
Looking back at the girl
Who still lives brightly inside my head.

In the summer I would wear yellow
And bare my shoulders to the sun and the moon,
Hoping to be noticed, and loved.
Who would now ask me into the garden at dusk
So the roses could look at me?

Would it be easier if I *felt* quite old?
Would my reflection then be a friend,
And not the stranger who stares back?
I *used* to be young, and sometimes pretty.

CHANGE

There has been a change; all of his walks, now, are with her,
And there is no lightness in her step as they climb the long
hill together.
She is impatient, calling as he tries to linger by a favourite
place
Sniffing the rich smells of fox or rabbit which he used to
chase;
The lead pulls, and he cannot wander;
The lead pulls, and she says "No time, no time".

Inside the house there are seldom voices;
She sits by that flickering screen and calls him to her,
Strokes him, holds his head in her lap.
He slips onto the once forbidden sofa.
But she warms her hands on his rough neck fur,
Buries her face in his rough neck fur,
And often her face is wet.

One day they hear again a motor, and he knows the man
Has returned. He feels her hand stiffen as she holds his col-
lar,
Then she allows the hand to loosen, and joyfully
Signalling welcome. It thumps as the man climbs up
through the garden
But the woman stands, frozen, waiting for the key to turn.
He would like to bound up to the man who enters, but feels
A tension that runs right through the space between them;
Though words are hushed and polite, the tones forbid entry
Into the space between them. Then his lady runs from the
room,
And the footsteps run upstairs where he may not follow.
And his man turns to him, and allows him to push his nose
in the hand
That so often caressed him. His man walks around the
rooms,
Taking things from shelves and placing them in boxes
That were stood in the hall, and often sighing,
Or stopping to caress the eager shadow that can't under-
stand the change.
He runs to the door, but his man
Takes him back to the room with the flickering screen
And onto the sofa that was once forbidden,
And warms his hands on the rough neck fur,
Buries his face in the rough neck fur,
And his face is wet.

Rebecca Jerrison

TRANSLATING THE PRACTICE

(To my father, and my father before him)

My real name is
Rebecca.
I do not know the
Sounds it is made of,
And I do not hear
The footsteps that
Walk away.

Tonight, I sit in silence;
A prayer for my brother,
Who died a long time
Ago, and I pray also for
The family who could not
Grieve his going, and I
Touch the jewishness of
His light that is shining still.

My real name is
Rebecca.
I sat with the soldiers
In Jerusalem,
And shared their wine
And song,
Like spilt blood
No longer laughing;
The eyes of boys
And men that owed their life
To machinery
And guns.

I too owe my life to
The footsteps I cannot hear,
And to the sounds
I don't yet know.
I too carry the machinery
Of seeds planted long ago,
When the violence and
Killing were all around me,
And my Father,
Unable to stop,
Raped me, before I
Could speak.

I too owe my life
To a momentary break of
Sunlight.
It kept a small child
Wanting, waiting, hoping.
Finally, out of the cupboard,
My spine still twisted
With pain,
I try to straighten,
Falter, fall and surrender.
One day I know I shall
Walk,
But for now, I crawl into
Peace,
And my tears prepare
The land for harvest.

Stella Jones

COMMUTER SERVICE

Take your clothes off
slowly.
Shake the greyness from your back.
Peel off the layers of your daytime.
Come to me.

Let us clean ourselves in a million bubbles
bursting on our bodies.
Let the water they're borne on
gurgle and laugh, as it plays us
riding from head to foot.

Glow with me.
Lie with me.
Let me bring you to life
my tongue, drinking the sweat, with you
drowning in my eyes.

Seeing neither stars nor moonlight
At day break - people break.
Where are the colours?
Red salt sand,
fields of all sorts ripening daily.

Hiding in their trains
Crashing in their cars,
Ashen
Who knows how they've made their homes?

DESAPARACIDOS

Sounds in the night.
Hammering on our door.
Screaming; crying.
Clothes torn
Struggling
A watch falling to stop,
Stop it all.

Guns in the air
Silent, waiting men,
Eyes wandering
Black boots clacking on stone.
Tyres screeching.

An empty room.
Upturned chairs.
The kitchen light is yellow on my sickness.
I look for you everywhere,
In dark corners where shadows move.
I am alone.

I am your memory.
I am your smile on cracked lips.
I am the tear that mingles with your sweat,
The hand that strikes you
Again and again.
I am sliding away.

The wind covers you
You lie with eyes closed
Perfectly still.

I walk the square
Your photo glued to my breast.

I keep searching.
There are no answers.

I will never find the grave that bears your name.

THE CAMPS

and so it came to pass
from skin-wrapped bones
thrown carelessly,
left to wither,
huge piles of waste,
poems and paintings were born.
God was pardoned for His sins.

I begat a word
you a shower of colours.

from the pit
particles of dust rose,
sailed skyward,
united,
joined forces with the sun.

lying in bed
some madness behind me, more to come
I wait to drown in dust particles.
they float
weaving down to cover me.

I am a believer
Re-born.

I drink dust juice
with my eyes.

Dorothy Judd

THE WASTED ONES

We let them sit in crumpled heaps
Ragbag clothes
Smell of stale jumble sale
Urine
And worse.
We let strangers
(in *loco infantis*)
Lift them,
Feed them,
Or, who knows,
Hurt them.
Aw right?
Aw right.

The whitefaced fragile folk
With paperthin skin
Can break
Easily
Easily we let them slip away
And then we are sorry.

GRANDFATHER

Barnacled brow
riveted jaw
seamed neck
Grandfather
fits into a shoebox
in my dream.

Don't play in the builders' sand
carries my mother's warning -
ringworms and worse.

Shoebox coffin
unearthed in the sand
lurking in corners of the toilet
and of my mind
for childhood years
and years.

New dolls come in shoeboxes,
pink and sweet-smelling
but not effacing
the yellowing of the wrinkled
man.

VICTORIA STATION: BEFORE COMMUTER CROWDS COME

Swaddled and swathed in layers of allsorts clothing,
She sits squarely on a bench,
Cushioned by bags of her travelling life,
Bags within bags bundled bulging
bags of all the babies she never had,
Statuesque as a Moore mother,
She wears her hope at the end of a ball of wool,
Knitting
A square
The colour of the promised day
Clean and baby fresh -
A patch of sky blue
In the grey morning quilt.

UPON THE DEATH OF A CHILD

The cup of sorrow overflows
Absorbed by the warm sand.

Pointed toe pirouettes,
Echoes the wet circle,
Etches the sand.

Silver aqueous sparks
Explode,
Iridescent, efflorescent.
Last flowering of one little girl,
Queen of the sea shore,
Brink of death,
Steeped in life.

Waves erase,
(Pas-de-chat, pas-de chat,)
Each wave different from the one before,
At the edge of this womb tomb.

Lila Julius

SUNFLOWERS

Field   bordering on the cemetery   a day
in Elul (August)   burnt   bent   blackened
we plough them under   after
the harvest   but lay the neighbour's boy   unboxed
a hollow stock   into the ground   before
his season   sunripe and shining.

PECAN PICKING

for Joanie

I help a friend pick pecans
in this unseasonable December
Sacks fill with black-streaked fruit
the wet and glossy newborns
plucked from yellow tulip husks
still on the trees
or camouflaged in leafy ground cover

Shirt-sleeved on garden chairs
our two heads bent above a barrelful
of last year's harvest, we sit
with fingers darkening
and give ourselves to crushing shells
and talk

A ritual develops: easy pace
a give and take of confidences
digging for the pith
The pail fills.

CALLIGRAPHY

I sift the raked sand of their papers
hoping to track my parents' script
catch figures that teetered in brown columns
crab legs skittering across a yellow page
my father's notebooks...
On his sixth birthday, fringes flapping
he took himself to school
refused to bare his head, went home.
He made his own lessons.

Our mother's hand was in rolling stock
a schoolgirl's script crossing blue-tracked pages
She liked a swept station, time-tables
sandwiches in transparent bags. Going places.
We waited on platforms for trains
that never came, or carried us off
in the wrong direction and always
on the lips of our questions
her gloved finger.

What I find are beaches
bathed traceless as a homeopathic potion
memory potent.

Lotte Kramer

THE TABLECLOTH

A tablecloth,
A white, coarse linen weave,
A dead thing, so it seems.
Its threads are gentle rent
In places, as in dreams,
When falling into pits
We wake in unbelief.

So frays this weft.
My father's mother made
The cloth in quiet days.
What patient thoughts she wove
Around this loom, narrow
Village ways, important
Hours underlined her shade.

Now, when I touch
This fragile web, and spread
It with our wine and bread,
And watch it slowly die,
I grieve not for its breach
But for the broken peace,
The rootlessness, our dread.

AUNT ELISE

My aunt Elise,
Daughter and sister of rabbis,
Was roundness incarnate.

111

Dripping with long-fringed shawl
And smelling of soap,
Of wax and wood,

She stood with the heat
In a low-beamed room
Of the black and white house:

The mothball wife
Pregnant with prayer
She curled her hands

And widened her eyes
Like frightened pennies:
Questioning her childlessness.

THE NON-EMIGRANT

(My father in Nazi Germany)

He left the application forms
Hidden inside his desk and missed
His quota for the USA.

He thought he'd stay and wait and stare
The madness out. It could not last.
He would not emigrate, not lose

His home, his language and his ground.
Beside his armchair sat a pile
Of books; the smoke from his cigar

Fenced comfort with a yellow screen.
His daily walk was all he'd need,
He thought. Abroad was where he'd been.

DEAD RHINE

That river cannot weep
Poison has starched his eyes
To a witches' frost of sleep.

Where once, a child, I slipped
Into his soft green silk
And loved the slimy steps

That led me down, now stand
The mourners coffin-deep
Watching the dry-eyed land

Lament a dark disease
That from some human hands
Flung devils to the trees,

The waters and their beasts.
Oh plunge your fists through fears
And find the ring that keeps
Tenure and faith with tears.

FOR COLETTE

Through her
I take possession
Of that long, hard gaze
To know
The scarlet pulse in men,
In plants, in animals,
To tell
The charm and misery
Of us: in love with love,
To hear
In summer's alphabet
The earth voice of a mother,
To melt
The yeast of memories,
Touch with my palm, my tongue,
My shin
Each unmet thought and taste,
Inhabit houses, new
At first,
Inherit libraries
Alive with dust and smell,
Declare
The movement of each limb
As pleasure's miracle.

Jane Liddell-King

DYING FOR JERUSALEM
(or perhaps for a fragrant bagel)

Here I am not among Jews
and G-d knows how I miss them
especially you Ida
catching the bus nearest Grodzinski's
your fifty-nine year old hair catching the sun
your nails perfectly trimmed to
plait the challah
Jane Liddell-KingI want to hear you talking
soup talking
fresh vermicelli for Benjamin
talking bagels
talking falafel
Warsaw talking
Jerusalem talking
English around you tasting wafer thin
flour dry
flaky
greytrollopey pathological posthumous necrophiliac

Home and now
Benjamin's eyes take you in
and beside him Miriam can't stop speaking
strudel
You put the fine art of filo pastry into and under her fingers
she is bursting with sultanas
between her teeth and clinging to her chin
this is the oldest of love's languages
Anni the children call you
Anni Mamma Manna
savouring
you

the chickens are boiling slowly
the juices clarify

Oh G-d Ida here in trappist city
where heads glance down from the frigid heights of reason
turreted windows towers spires
locked places
courts conceived by stone cerebra
knot gardens
memento mori

and hands
which won't touch and eyes
which can't wait to meet the Siberian distance
getting to grips only with
the consolation of the past
or the unimaginable theory of Black Holes
Ida I want you
blessjng the bread
blessing the candles
talking Festival
talking Adela Anna Genia David
and all theirs
talking Jericho
then and now
secretly relishing my dream of kissing Arafat
talking the six million
the valley of the shadow
talking cheesecake
talking cream
saying
Gut Shabbas
Li Chaim
and next year
home at last
liebchen
this I promise you

London
New York
and Jerusalem.

POST-COITUM

for Freyja

She has his head in her hands
his thigh touches hers
certainly the earth has moved
and she has held the universe in her palm
witnessed the very beginning of time
and the room was wild with fireworks
fireworks and chrysanthemums
but now how she craves sleep
only something she has said has roused him
touched him with the first frail shoot
of a wickedly green idea
his mind's on the loose again
amazed at its feats at 2.00 a.m.
the red arrows had certainly better look out
people he says
people and stories
stories and history
so who shapes what
and what whom
and is there a significant difference
every orgasm
has its own colour
whatever the pathologist neurologist sexologist
would have us make believe
and tonight IS different from all others
to cap it all he reaches for his Wittgenstein and says

if this is the answer what is the question
but she longing to keep the peace
kisses him quiet again
if only she can presume that like her he's heard
that
in the beginning
there wasn't a word

*Please feel free to substitute Gertrude Stein for Wittgenstein
or any other stein of your choice. Far be it from me to leave
any stein unturned.*

SCIENCE AND INDUSTRY

You call me a survivor
and your voice creams its admiration
you say
such lovely children
the sweetest husband on the block
the smartest apartment
and a real success at work
your bathwear has always been irresistible

Chani you got it wrong
these 50 years of ersatz life
of Khaddish life
of fostering Arni's children
oh ja his sons and mine
but me
a changeling mother
hunched in a cold skin

I can tell you
the moment she died
Elzbieta Chazan
at twenty-two
Rahel in her arms
I remember
Rahel
and Josef lulling her to sleep
so
Li li li li li li li li li li
so she wouldn't be heard
her sharp new cry which rose over
the whispering of the girls
and the old men grunting
in that light sleep
snatched when they were worn out with prayers
she hadn't tasted milk
it hadn't come
not by the night they came to Kovno
and took us to the air field
Rahel clutched in Elzbieta's skinny arms
tight under her coat
and then
just off the sweat-filled bus
she struggled suddenly to fill her lungs
with open air
a shock to her
and how she needed
to suck
knew
the milk was coming
wanted
to unclench and see her hands
the mother felt the newborn spine uncurl
her hurting womb about to spill

Was hast du da?
the soldier said
du hast etwas doch
das weiss ich
Was ist?
Zu essen nicht?
Nun gibt die Bundel hier
Nu said Elzbieta
then ach Chani then
what happened then
what was she thinking of
what did her wooden limbs do
would this man soften if he saw
the child
the miraculous blonde hair
she stood all fear
Chani
she held out her aching arms
her waking child
whom he roughly took
such greed in his eyes
and then he went further and further
into the fighting air
smaller and smaller
among
the staggering bus loads
the stretching queues

the waiting trains

blood crept down her legs
her blank body stood there stung
by its first milk drop
the swelling breasts hurting
like secondary tumours
and this survivor died
in silence

but Chani
they never buried her

Sonja Lyndon

REMEMBERING THE OLD COUNTRY

I live in another country now,
And day by day I am a pillar of salt
Licked by the furry tongues of beasts
Who lap me until night time comes.
But when the moon and all her stars
Glow down upon my crystal frame,
Thin-waisted as an hour glass,
She casts a shadow pencil slim
That stretches to the hinderland
Behind my back.
All through the night I elongate
Until the mournful moment when
I cross the scarlet frontier line
In black relief.
And in the still electric air
My dark self lies on stony ground
Caught on the wire, barbed and fixed
A ridge of scars above my hips
Stigmata to be lanternlit
By moon and stars. And all because
I live in another country now.

ADAMAH

I am a soft woman
Come strike me with your spade
Press down with your foot
So the hard straight blade
Slides down through my flesh
Cutting straight past my skin
And with one small push
You sink right in
While the sound of the breeze
Is my only breath
As with effortless ease
You slice through the loam
No shock of rock
Or flinty bone
To block your way
So you can journey
Endlessly
On a path that takes you
Straight through me
For loam is soft
And yields like foam
It has no shape to call its own
And that is why you love and hate
This soft woman.

INVESTMENT

Each meal, each smile, each tin of paint,
Each joke the second time around,
Each handle turned, each sleeve rolled up,
Each time the light goes out at night,
Each hiss of steam from kettled chrome,
Each stroke of naked foot on foot,
Each sound of joy, each News at Ten,
Each sticky moment to be passed,
Each clash of moods, each lightbulb changed,
Each vase that's filled, each watered pot,
Each bath that's run and then run out,
Each change of clothes, each hair that falls,
Each window opened to be closed,
Each strawberry hulled, each crocus spied,
Each journeying out to journey back,
Each telephone message to be passed,
Each glass of wine or two or three,
Each flushing down the lavatory bowl,
Each picture hammered on the wall,
Each letter posted, table wiped,
Each drawer that's opened, stair that's climbed,
Each word that's spoken, coat removed,
Each sock that's washed, each floor that's cleaned,
Each bill that's paid, each tear that's shed,
Each arch of back, each roll of hip,
Each "each" that passes with each day,
Each time I lie,
Each time you say...
Each time we do...
Each...

Rochelle Mass

CHILDHOOD LOST

a broken wrist
a snake bitten foot
a bruised back
inflamed ovarian tubes
cysted breast
pills taken
stomach pumped
before she was fifteen

she left school
no
teachers
no
homework
then
no
army

men
both
black and white
lay in her bed
smoke and dirty cups
music and musty love
poems and books
she read and wrote

she wasn't home
long enough
now she is
and so am i
partners in the void
a childhood lost
and
a daughter found

LIKE A COMPASS BOUND FOR NORTH

Some men walk with thick thighs
and flat feet
growl commands
take only what they want with yellowed hands
with dull eyes they stare down their prey

Some men walk with soft steps
meeting lovers on the way
offering warmth like a compass
bound for north

They stroke a woman's neck
shaking doubts from her lips
placing jewels on her eyes

IN THE SAME ROOM

My grandfather died when
i was six
his bladder wrapped in choking
cells that kept him in a hospital room
crowded with other moaning grey men
i lay awake for seven days
in a dark room
listening to early morning prayers
shiva for the dead
and fell to sleep each of the seven
hearing the drone of men
with black head circles
and striped shoulder shawls
facing east to mourn this man

years later in that same room
i waited for my mother
who had the same sick cells around her colon
i waited as a girl of twelve this time
and in those waiting hours
in the same dark room
red flushes of hot blood
stormed through my legs
slashing my Babba's sheets
with flaming stains

one time in that dark room
i lost my grandfather
another i lost my childhood
these losses connected
as the menstrual monthly rolled
up my back and pinched my legs
pads and pins on a thin belt
twisted under my belly
harnessing the woman
i'd become
in that room

my grandfather died
in that room
i became a woman there
my mother lives

TONIGHT

Tonight
a new length of woman
is hatched
the night
drops burgundy petals
into her lap
tonight
her white skin
parades into
the moon's long shadow
the night
covers her hips
with threads
of red silk

LAST WORDS

he didn't want her perfume on his back
only to lie in the breath of her thigh
twist into the heat of her chest
he took no perfume on his arm
only the grain of her cheek
and the last words she gave him
he held in his palm during nights
when he was cold
and she in another man's bed

Gerda Mayer

MAKE BELIEVE

Say I were not sixty,
say you weren't near-hundred,
say you were alive.
Say my verse was read
in some distant country,
and say you were idly turning the pages:

The blood washed from your shirt,
the tears from your eyes,
the earth from your bones;
neither missing since 1940,
nor dead as reported later
by a friend of a friend of a friend...

Quite dapper you stand in that bookshop
and chance upon my clues.

That is why at sixty
when some publisher asks me
for biographical details,
I still carefully give
the year of my birth,
the name of my hometown:

GERDA MAYER born '27, in Karlsbad,
Czechoslovakia...write to me, father.

*Note: The author's father, Arnold Stein, escaped from the
German concentration camp in Nisko in 1939, fled to
Russian-occupied Lemberg/Lwow, and then disappeared in
the summer of 1940. It is thought he may have died in a
Russian camp.*

THE EMIGRATION GAME (WINTER 1938/39)

Mother and I walk through the streets of Prague.
Her hands are balled against the falling snow.
(Can't she afford gloves? Are they bare from choice?)
There's snow above and endless steps below.

We have a bag of chocolate-creams; we play
The emigration game: England, if brown;
Or, if the centre's white, we must stay here;
If yellow, it's Australia. Snow falls down.

I pick a brown and mother has the white.
She walks with a straight back: Let's try again.
Her legs are varicosed; her heels are raised.
She's bearing up and stout of heart. In vain

From consulate to consulate her steps
Inscribe petitions. Soon the sweets are gone.
Then March comes and invaders bar all routes:
Yet leave no trace of her when they move on;

Their footsteps beating time and bearing down.

ANON

I was resting my feet between two pogroms
And cooling them in a stream,
When through the tender leaves above
I saw an angel gleam.

My guardian angel: I knew him at once.
He floated about the tree.
Now carry me off and carry me high.
And he said *presently.*

And presently means by-and-by,
And by-and-by, anon.
He settled his halo and flapped his wings;
He kissed me and was gone.

IN HIS ORCHARD

In his orchard of little ripe corpses
The giant walked one day
And the little wind in the branches
Carried the stench away:

Carried it over the fencing
Of skeletons linking arms,
Where Lieschen and Gretchen were dawdling,
Surveying the orchard's charms.

They did not weep for the dead men
Bobbing in the trees,
They did not weep for their hungry eyes,
They did not weep for these.

They were nice, blonde, natural girls,
And when the smell arose
From where the giant was striding,
Each giggled and held her nose.

Between dances and beer that evening,
Said Gretchen, raising her drink:
No wonder he had to hang them;
They absolutely stink.

Pamela Melnikoff

FOR A CHILD NOT YET CONCEIVED

Your room awaits you, and a cherry-tree
That never bloomed till now: and clematis
Purpling the kitchen wall; and ancestors
Whose faith and kindness reach out down the years
To touch you with their light; and happy friends;
And books and music, art and poetry
And all the precious and God-given things
That we have found and hoarded for your sake;
And aunts and cousins; and a squalling nest
Under the eaves; and daisies in the grass;
Laughter and love, legend and fantasy,
And such a welcome as the flowers of March
And every blessing sent to make men glad
And all the saints and prophets never had.

Why do you linger still, then, in that sad
Populous kingdom where our lost dreams are,
Ungathered fruit and every unborn thing?
The years are passing, and we pass likewise
And cannot wait forever on your whim.
You must come soon, or you may wait too long
And come too late, and find the hearth grown cold,
The windows shuttered, and your parents old.

Sarah, they say, laughed when the angel told
How she, at ninety years of age, would bring
A shining son out of her shrivelled womb,
And would my laughter, do you think, be less;
My miracle, and my sweet thankfulness?

BURNT OFFERING (A SONG OF AUSCHWITZ)

Today is Passover, a time once made
Festive with prayer and with burnt offerings.
We shall have both before the day is out.

In bible times our fabled ancestors
Came with their flutes over the singing hills
To make obeisance in Jerusalem,
Their robes like morning milk, their languorous harps
Golden as honey, heavy with the hum
Of leaves and fountains and the doves of peace.
And with them came the chosen sacrifice,
Speechless and garlanded, with gilded horns.

All this is history, long time forgotten,
Preserved in ancient scrolls, in tattered prayerbooks,
Or is it just a dream that we are dreaming?

In those days there was sunlight on the mountains,
Drums in the meadows, shining green hosannas,
Vineyards and olives, joy and benediction.
Then each deluded Hebrew loved his neighbour.
We brought you living flesh. Gladly we gave it,
And the smoke went up to Heaven among the cymbals.

Now the great chimney-stack obscenely lolls
Across the molten sky, gorged with strange flesh
And spewing sacred smoke this festive day,
And who shall be the chosen sacrifice?
We are the Paschal lamb and the dumb ox
Slaughtered without the benison of flowers.
The blood we spill before you is our blood.
On altar-stones our shattered bones are burning.

O God, who never since the world began
Let the miraculous pattern of our birth
Slip from your mind; who never once forgot
To call the migrant swallow home again
Or set the moth free from his chrysalis;
Who never left the cursed and treacherous snake
To starve; whose memory does not forget
The smallest trusting leaf waiting for Spring,
Have you forgotten our old covenant,
The flutes and cymbals and the gilded horns,
The chosen sacrifice, so gladly given,
The voices praising you, and all the singing?

Joan Michelson

STORY BLOCK: BOGDAN 196-

this is a story about bogdan he lives in new york
new york the u n finds his tongue useful
he is writing a play about warsaw each day he eats
and the germans fruitcake on broadway he cannot stop
talking   he remembers his childhood and cousins
he speaks of one thousand dollars his head is large
and a femme fatale in paris he is short and thick
who was a person and not a sex object   his arms are bone
he cannot stop talking he hates the american woman
nor biting his thumb nails and of course hypocrisy
one girl insisted on the floor   she said her bed
was for the man she loved bogdan was not
the professor looked the other way when he
bogdan hates the professor his eyes are flecked with green
his secretary is practically naked   he must rent a machine
and living with a man he must rent an inexpensive
his landlady is her mother tape recorder   he is going
people he knows constantly avoid him he will never return
they walk in the opposite after he has finished
he is flying to europe this assignment this thursday
she said she loves only bearded cabbies over fifty
nothing can shock him all females are crazy
he is writing a play he must take his pants to the cleaners
about two children writing an essay in warsaw   he is
thirty-six nixon has just been elected he translates
from english into polish and german american president
his briefcase is bumping the hudson is rising
a gun goes off he cannot stop talking   he must
on thursday sirens are screaming   bogdan lives in new york

UNEARTHLY FLOOD

I carry the bleached skull home
from the ghetto grounds,
and dig a hole
It was a Jewish dog.

I visit Auschwitz on the 26th,
return to Holland on the 28th.
The Rhine at Lobith is fifty five feet
above the sea. It's fifty years
since the Russians found my cousins
among the skeletons.

Lamentations have been broadcast
all this month. "We the living have to tell".
He packed one bag; roped his bedroll.
Under his floorboards, he buried his gold.

The rivers are surging in high winds, -
the Waal, the Maas, the Rhine, the Main,
as if to bring the sky down for mourning.
Can the God of Forgiveness stop
this loss?

From Moscow an architect shows us
blueprints for double brick ovens.
Then drawings of slides to the cellar
for an ever-increasing number.

Imagine one million chickens, six hundred
thousand cows, slaughtered pigs,
rats in the crumbling dikes,
goats, birds, snakes, feral cats.
Then add the lost Jews.

The dog's skull rained dirt on my hands.
Vines twisted like wire above the graves.
The stones were broken and choked to the top
of the carved words.

This sky enters the mudded earth
and pauses without remorse.
It leaves me no voice for singing;
not even when the sun flies out
like a psalm after all.

Rena Minkoff

ALTE ZACHEN

"Old things" he cried, "bring out
your old things. Old things I buy.
Shoes, clothes, towels, hats,
Furniture, refrigerators, stoves."
- And put all that
In his little wagon, and rolled off,
Yelling for more.

He used to come with cart and mule.
We knew his days, and how
He'd finger and poke our small
castoffs, and shrug and offer nothing -
Or near to nothing as we'd take.

We moved house. He smelled it out.
"Alte" he yelled, bashing
at my door, window, wall, while
I cowered in a corner by the table.
He never budged. "Old things, old"
He wheedled, putting the fear of God in me.

To shut him up I let him in at last.
And there he was, looking, prodding,
Grunting at the paucity of gain.
"How much, how much?" always, everything, twice.
And the mule forlornly drooped its head.
Cupboard, ice-box, mouldy jars,
A pittance for the lot.
Anger grew with fear, and when he asked
"Why take so long to open?"
I screamed with rage until he left.

He comes now in a motor van.
His voice, amplified, echoes
Through streets and forests, thunders off the hills.
"I buy, I buy", again the list,
"Furniture, refrigerators, stoves,
Clothes, bottles, books,
Bicycles, irons, electricals. Old things, old."

Locked in his cart he has, perhaps,
The wall of the temple, a stone from Absalom's tomb;
A scroll from the Dead Sea, and Moses' staff;
Two Greek sarcophagi, Elijah's mantle.
Angels gather nightly in his yard.
Shrouds and cerements gleam
As he burns old things, old things.

Malakh haMavet - Angel of Death -
He'll come for me.

Lilian Mohin

ETCHING

traces, fine bird prints
above the tide line

do the grains of sand recall
compressing tight to make that shape

or loosening in the new arrangement?

even after waves, somewhere,
my cells remember how it was

your track etching.

Cheryl Moskowitz

SURRENDER

So, breathing a sigh
she said surrender
and the soft rain poured down on a city
where life was never still
and into the room
some of its turbulence seeped through
the cracks in the ceiling
and gaps in the windows
and spilled on to the floor where her clothes lay
bundled in a heap
of hurried and unrestrained caress,
yes, and still more
the angry ticking from the clock face
mirrored traffic noises, flooding gutters
spraying kerbs and pavements and autobahns
awake with night muscle and brawn
it ticked into her crevices
where the soft nothingness of letting go
had only just started to find a bed.

It clawed and scratched its way
into technicolour fantasies of woven pastures
knitted with flying hills
and valleys
and white winged soldiers of love.

It pummelled and fought its way inside
until her sigh was only a whisper
and then, not even that
and the raindrops, she could see,
had left a nasty stain on the window pane
I'll have to see to that
she thought
and left abandonment behind.

No place for late night sighing
of surrender here
the day cracks through the night
and she remembers
she is supposed to fight
and so joins chorus with the dawn birds' song
that won't give up.

PASSING MEN

Certain things make my skin stand on end
my back prickle
the kind of fear a dog can smell;
A sort of panic.
Passing men in tight places
passing men at all, in fact

I remember you in your study, Daddy
red hair, freckled neck pouring over *Scientific American*
back issues bound to come in useful
boxes and boxes in the storeroom
and a stethoscope or two
so you
could hear me coming when I tiptoed past
the open passageway
and shout out, Hey
What makes you so afraid, little girl?
Wielding your Adam's gavel loud and long.

The kind of shout that lodges fingers in a throat
or perches inside teeth to make a wolf whistle stand out
on dusty nights
construction sites

I never did like passing men
It was the luminous lust that smelled like pus
from leering eyes
that left me cold
so cold that I forgot to turn and wave
a gesture of defiance
in their animal hungry faces
turned in rubber unison
pathetically erect, to watch
the swirling skirt
the clicking heels
the can't-have-want-more sway of their sultry hips
my hips

"A little lady", you said
A young woman
projecting tiny peaks from her cotton t-shirt like a prize.

Pat the bottom, Daddy - while it's yours to pat.
Soon the street will lay their claims
Now what do you think of that?

MOTHER

You gave me these lips,
Mother
and I wanted to use them
to say it was your fault -

So that nothing I could do would hurt.

A gentle wind carries my words high
a breeze
I can't be touched.
I wanted to blame you with my mouth
so you could use yours
to kiss away the tears.

GRANDMA

I thought I had left it too late,
feared it so.
That I might have let the ticking of time
and the silence of years
drain away anything to do with my past.
It was her food, her cooking I remember most.
No,
perhaps her eyes awash with unshed tears
and her long hair
down to her waist and whiter than
a dove's wing.
It was everything.
She was the grandma I would write stories about.
Her life was a story
I wanted told to me
again and again so I could attach
her history to my own
and anchor my Eastern European looks
and name with pride
in a land of Howard Johnson's
and Captain Kangaroo.

But you told me she is not gone.
I had feared it would be so
and that my not hearing
not knowing, not seeing for so long
would have dissolved her -
white granules disappearing into clear water.

She is ninety-four you say
and smiles at the nurses who look after her.
Ninety-four
Well, I do not suppose they make you
matzo balls, Grandma, where you are
or stuff cabbage leaves like you did in your kitchen
with two sets of everything.

146

I have an apple tree in my garden now too
and sometimes I sit and pare apples
cutting them into great chunks like you did
soaking them in salt water for preserving.

The peel and core I throw away.
This will rot in time
leaving only the flesh
only flesh

that we share
and to know you are still there
in the flesh and smiling
makes my heart ache with gladness
and my flesh
the flesh that we share
tingle with hope.

Danielle Nagler

LEDOR VADOR

You ask, my child (that was not)
Why I sit alone this afternoon,
Watching a grey sky shuffle past
Dusty windows on an English Sunday.
In the silence, the empty house
Sighs for you (that was not),
Barren walls shivering in their nakedness
Without a photograph to clutch to pale breasts.

And I in a single rocking chair
Think on you (that was not),
And on him, that was and so soon not,
Yet might have been, who knows...
A boy who changed
His chocolate for a bright canary
And left me, with his other women,
When we were five, and love
Was not a thing declared.

I glimpsed the page of history that said
Age twenty-one we married, lived
In the wooden house on the edge of town,
And you (that was not) would be two years later.
But the winter skies, when we were five,
Were leaden heavy sweeping between the hedges,
Driving ahead a flock of might have beens
In sagging clouds that did not burst in sight.
While I stared through dirty windows,
At a passing canary, chocolate melting in my hands.

You ask, my child (that was not)
Why I sit alone this afternoon,
Watching a grey sky shuffle past
Dusty windows on an English Sunday.
In the silence a far off radio laments,
Carried on a festering Eastern wind;
My mind paces across empty years survived,
Blank spaces for you, that was not.

Linda Rose Parkes

SEDER EVE

"He who is hungry, come and eat.
He who is needy, come and join our pesach".

We have laid a place for the unknown guest.
On the table a bowl of ground almonds,
Boiled egg, fresh horseradish for the bitter herb,
black grapes. Wafting in from the kitchen
is the smell of cholent.

The children are red cheeked
dipping matzos into watered wine.
We stammer prayers from the Haggadah
in this first year of our mother's widowhood,
her grief's long journey.

As the youngest gets up
to open the door for the pilgrim
hope startles us -
Planted before you died,
are the climbing yellow roses;
rocked by the tide, their steady breathing.

TRILOGY

I. Snorkeling in the red sea with my sister

It takes me ages to fix my mask and snorkel.
You're busy with your ten pound underwater camera
trying to get a shot of the lion fish and the
Emperor Angel.

150

It distracts you that I stick so close as if I was
only eight and you had my bus ticket.
Imagine staying down here with the pulsating
sea urchins the brain coral so silent.

You as the Masked Butterfly with lots of yellow.
me as the cubic-headed Picasso Trigger fish.

We could leave the roped-off sea paths,
Visit the souls of pharaoh's horses, leisurely now
in all their movements, the thumb-size sea horses.

We could swim to Jordan, Egypt, without passports.
Find that narrow path perhaps between parted water;
the Jewish half of ourselves coming towards us.

II. Homeland

After long security delays and flooding,
the coach edges past rubble, deserted tanks,
each drop illuminated in the headlamps.

The coloured lights of Aqaba remind me of my
native Jersey coastline.
But my ignorance confounds me.

A book on Israel, a Hebrew phrase book, a few
salty herrings of grandma's Yiddish.
Jordan on the left, Egypt on the right.

Having let go of roots
I come face to face with paradox....
the kipa I've chosen for my half-Jewish
lover; the one for my son being brought up
Catholic.

And knowing how my mother wishes she had made
her home here, away from the taboos of her Anglo-
smart set.
Unorthodox Jewish-
remembering the breath of unbrushed teeth
in the Synagogue of childhood-

it soothes her to hear local entertainers
croon English, American show songs under lit
date trees.
A different language at every table.

III. Samuel's christening

Standing in the pew clutching a hymn book
takes me back to school when I knew the hymns
in English, could belt them out with the
best of the Gentiles.

I look at my son sitting across the aisle
with his classmates
Last Friday we celebrated Sabbath
kipa perched on his head short of a kirbigrip.

The jumper I bought him for today is two sizes
too big, arms rolled up.
He's bathed and washed his hair
his shoes have been polished.

In front of me is a statue of the Virgin Mary
with the baby Jesus.
I wonder how thick the gold is, how deep you'd have
to dig before reaching plaster.

She must have loved her little boy's cuddles as much
as any mother.
What was it he said to her, het up and frightened
by the time she found him in the temple?
"Did you not know I was in the house of my father?"

Soon the priest's long fingers will draw the cross
on my son's lovely forehead where I've planted kisses.
Tip the jug Im Namen des Vaters, des Sohnes
und des Heiligen Geistes.

He knows I'm only going along with his father's wishes.
Now he looks at me, needs the crowning of his mother's
blessing.

Sylvia Paskin

WONWELL BEACH/ AGAIN

He reached inside, took
it from where it lay
half-buried, among the spindly
apricot crabs, tongued wet
grains of sand away, and
burnished it with sunlight

unfolded cunning fingers

so it was revealed in
his pale, narrow palm,
quartz and agate, deeply
veined, pocked and scarred,
a heart of stone -
not to be found again

MAD SHE WAS AND CRAZY

White silk dress with huge
Red roses bobbed on long green
Ambling stems. Anglo-Indian,
She was very lovely -
Dorothy has come to stay.

And the great ape beside her
A minder from the Soho club
Pulled her shoulder
Pulled her haunches
Pulled no punches in
What he said -

Where is he you'll need protection
Where is he she hissed your father
Tell him that I want him now.

Blood on dress same as roses
She smiles a razor in one hand
Wrists are slit and stitched
And bandaged just a hint
Of agony -

Sumptuous, swaying
A tattered Jaiphur ruby
Oh my father

He was her (tor)mentor
Daughter-figure here
transfigured and for God's
sake what was I -

THE OPEN HEART

I am not one voice
but many
what I hold is
fire
in the beating of my heart

I am not one voice
but many
what I fear is
silence
in the lying of my heart

I am not one voice
but many
what I touch is
crystal
in the breaking of my heart

I am not one voice
but many
what I hear is
stillness
in the greening of my heart

I am not one voice
but many
what I crave is
Eden
in the dreaming of my heart

I am not one voice
but many
what I know is
love
in the opening of my heart

Alix Pirani

DRY LADIES

Be dry, said her mother, always dry.
Don't wet yourself. Don't cry.
So she was dry all her life, very dry:
Her wit,
Her vagina,
And her clear blue eye.
She sat very still on dry ground
And dabbled one finger in a trickle of life.

One day the great flood came and knocked her over, easily.

She raged with surprise and fought and beat her fists
against the walls of water
Shouting "Get off me! How dare you!"
But her voice gurgled unheard amid the swirls of water
roaring about her, pushing around her.

She was so angry she cried.
She was so frightened she pee'd
And her wetness poured out of her
And she floated helpless.
Liquid, she was mingled with the waters,
Carried with the flood: turning, tumbling.

And now she flows, bewildered, with the great polluted river
of life.

Her mother is still sitting dry-eyed on the shore.

MARRYING IN AND OUT

Inside the warm ghetto suffocation
And outside the cold world of embracing
At arms' length
Their hands fumble toward my pain
And take my riches.

Inside the knife-twist of racial memory
And outside the haven of a landlocked history
The relief of diffused identity.

And between, the no-man's land
Is woman's land, where the torn womb
Rapturously bears its child
Into an estranged world
And longs to have it back again.

Anne Ranasinghe

UNTITLED

For Rosemary - July 1992

"Sei allem Abschied voran, als wäre er hinter Dir"[*]

Such a calm afternoon. A benign sun
greens the needles of monumental firs.
Below the meadow glitters the lake

where a male swan glides in regal style
guiding his cygnets, a downy single file.
And you tell the story of the mother swan

who died, poisoned, while still hatching her young.
Tea-time. We pass the cake. Your face
is pale, but beautiful, almost unchanged.

A family circle. We have gathered at this summery place
coming from far. It was arranged.
White linen, old china - and you, a hostess full of grace.

And a guest comes and joins us at the table,
we see him but we do not greet him,
and all the while he sits silently.

The afternoon softens into dusk
and the firs cast shadows that blacken and grow
towards a winter, a bitter winter

towards a winter that you will not know.
You are fragile as crystal, but also strong -
we talk lightly. It will not be long.

* *Be ahead of all parting, as though it already*
were behind you   Rilke, Sonnets to Orpheus

AUSCHWITZ FROM COLOMBO

Colombo. March. The city white fire
That pours through vehement trees burst into flame,
And only a faint but searing wind
Stirring the dust
From relics of foreign invaders, thrown
On this far littoral by chance or greed,
Their stray memorial the odd word mispronounced,
A book of laws
A pile of stones
Or maybe some vile deed.

Once there was another city; but there
It was cold - the trees leafless
And already thin ice on the lake.
It was that winter
Snow hard upon the early morning street
And frost flowers carved in hostile window panes

It was that winter.
Yet only yesterday
Half a world away and twenty-five years later
I learn of the narrow corridor
And at the end a hole, four feet by four
Through which they pushed them all - the children too
Straight down a shaft of steel thirteen feet long

160

And dark and icy cold
Onto the concrete floor of what they called
The strangling room. Dear God, the strangling room,
Where they were stunned - the children too -
By heavy wooden mallets,
Garroted, and then impaled
On pointed iron hooks.

I am glad of the unechoing street
Burnt white in the heat of many tropical years
For the mind, no longer sharp,
Seared by the tropical sun
Skims over the surface of things
Like the wind
That stirs but slightly the ancient dust

YOU, FATHER
From and old photograph

You, father, stand in your heavy dark coat
Against the winter tree. Ice on the lake,
And two small ducks that were caught afloat
By winter, frozen. The sun is behind me as I take
This photograph, and what I make
Is a last sad record, though I could not have known.

The sun behind me is cold and white
And projects my elongated shadow.
It falls black between us, yet lies so light
On the innocent, powdery snow.
You do not smile - is the sun in your eyes?
Or - now I wonder - could you have known?

ATTERIYA

Even through the closed windows it seeps on this Nikini
Poya night,
A scent so drenching that it drowns the senses. I open the
door
to the moon-washed garden - such stillness under the golden
light
of the huge Poya moon, all branches and leaves immobile -
searching for Atteriya, Queen of the Night,
and find it, tangled, by the side of the wall, its deep green
leaves
luminous in the moonlight and covered with delicate curling
white-petalled blossoms whose centres support their yellow-
tipped stamens.

The scent flows from the arched canopy, wave after wave,
flooding memory, awakening desire. I raise my hand to
touch
the tracery of leaves, and a shower of blossoms rains upon
me;
the ground is covered as with snow;
and I remember the words of Asclepiades
that the joys of the love goddess are to be found only among
the living
and that we shall all lie as no more than dust and bone
in the place of the dead.

Azila Reisenberger

NE'ILA

Chill the handle to the touch
Hesitates under the pressure of my palm.
Warm the room;
A caressing glance -
A dishevelled Bed.

Cold the handle to the touch
Slowly gives, slides down.
Warm the room;
Watchful glance -
A tattered doll.

Dry the handle to the touch
Draw the latch behind it.
Warm the room;
One last look -
A faded photograph.

Frozen the handle to the touch
The door yields, opens.
A Violent wind bursts in -
Smites the four corners -
I alone escape...

HERITAGE

The robe which I have inherited
from my parents
Hangs
In the entrance hall.
Still,
I am too small to reach it.

WOMEN IN LOVE

(To R. who bared her soul)

My Sister, My Bride,
My Sister, My Love,
His sinewy bulk
I gladly exchange
For your sunkissed Softness.
In the Womb of the night
Under a quilt of darkness
When you stretch out your hand to touch me
I strip off the cover,
The cover of Shame -
that cloaks us.

Sibyl Ruth

THE HOTHOUSE

Us kids.
With our crop of forced results.

Back home among boilers
radiators
double-glazed air
cavity installation.

That microclimate.

Mum by the cooker
where she stews and fries.
Giving my Dad *a nice secure feeling*.

Big brother
little brother.
All smiles
like pumpkins at the table.

They put us into separate pots.
Our weeded rooms.

Nobody ever said the word *darling*.

I hug my bottle
stand by the kettle.
Frostbitten.

CONTRACT

You're not to shout
or run stamping up the stairs
or stick your elbows out.

Food and accommodation will be provided.

You will learn your lesson,
ask permission.

Occasional sulking
and cries from a locked room
can be allowed.

You are to curb your body.
You'll be sorry.

Warnings will stay on your file.

You're going to simmer down,
tell anyone who asks, you're fine.

There's no review,
no appeals procedure.
Your case will not be heard by a tribunal.

It's entirely up to you.

This is our last offer.
Put your name on the dotted line..............

Deborah Sacks

HAVDALLAH

*Blessed art thou who hast made a distinction between the
sacred and the profane, between light and darkness, between
Israel and the other nations.*

I read the blessing and consider
The degree of my subversion

These rituals are alien to you.

The wax that falls on our hands
Cools into petals

Entwined, we burn with plural flame.

YOU OFFER ME RED APPLES

You offer me red apples
No thank you, I say
I want the fruit that is just out of reach
And tastes like nothing on earth.

Like nothing on earth, you say to me
Then come take my hand, you say.

167

THOUGH I COME TO YOU AT HARVEST

Though I come to you at harvest
Do not wait

Though I may weep with desire
Do not turn

For the eagle must be taught to be tamed
Or the thunder to break
And in fields of gentleness
I understood nothing but want.

Do not shine on me at harvest
Darling boy

Do not look at me

If I come to you
Do not turn

Requite me in kind.

Eva Salzman

COMING TO BED

When you exhale
one final cigarette
and its last smoke drifts,
dies into the furniture,
the day shuts down.
Only then
when the last notes
of music evaporate
with the thinking voice,
with persistence
and choice...only then
do you slip gently
out of the gravity
of consciousness
into a weightless
sphere of sleep.

I'm already asleep,
airing crops,
and you come down
to meet me in this pasture
that rolls in all directions,
where flowers of ideas
shimmer ghostlike,
seed stars nestled deep
in a carpet of clover
sloping up to sky,
far and near,
where the solid bitter sea
tilts, pours into ambiguity
of green, pales, then dissipates...

I know
when you arrive;
all meadows
like a scarf
roll up
from the corners
and reassemble
as my form
at your point of entry.
Then we wander off
in separate parts,
side-by-side,

until morning unfolds us
and daylight
breaks us away

CONCH

My grandmother doesn't hear me call; a white mist licks
her skull. She shuffles out to the jungle-yard
to pin a single greying cloth to the drying rack's
sun-dial spines, the dulling weather-vane
where the fading laundry's years have swung and aired.

The piece of washing turns its only two pages
back and forth, re-read by the wind, water veins
mapping the ground, while shadows throw vaguer
and vaguer epitaphs across the sheets snapping in the
breeze.
The woman goes inside, and her door shuts again
into the memory I'll always hold of its splintered frieze.

But my real grandmother's sealed thousands of miles away
in her red-brick house deafened with treasure - bone-and-
tulle
dancing skirts, dried quills, the family of bells
lined up in ever-decreasing size, their peals subsiding
to white noise, her shell collection emptying the sea,
vowels bleached on another shore; and from the countless
shelves
she's taken her umpteenth book to read in bed, yearning
for me, for the children, her ears burning.

THE REFINERY

You cannot look at narrow-brush moustaches.
You cannot think about gas-cookers, their ovens
flame-rimmed, the diadem of fire, or hear the bell
when it's done. Or think of teeth, lamp-shades, soap
the refinery chimney-stacks, puffing cheerfully.

You cannot raise your hand in history class
to ask a simple question; your arm freezes
in a parody of salute. You cannot write "horror"
because horror is a good film for anyone
with a strong stomach and a taste for gore.

Anyway, the antique photographs are grainy,
have blurred into art - that vaseline trick with the lens.

At dinner you sip the rot-gut wine
and listen to the table-talk - an operation botched
or an ache in the joints the doctor couldn't diagnose.
You choke with rage at the meal, gibbering,
while the devil samples your soul like buttered croissant.

171

Elizabeth Sarah

MEDITATION FOR TEFILLIN

I cannot
bind myself
to You
I can only
unbind myself
continually and
free
Your spirit
within me

So why
this tender-cruel
parody of
bondage
black
leather
straps
skin
gut and
sacred litany of
power and
submission
which binds us
Your slave-people
still?

My own answer is
wound around
with every
taut
binding and
unbinding
blood rushing
heart pounding
life-force surging
          pushing
          panting
          straining
          struggling to
          break through
          to You

Blessed are You, our Living God, Sovereign-Presence of the
Universe, whose commandments make us holy and who com-
mands us to lay tefillin.

APPROACHING THE END

Suffused with sadness
and an aching loneliness
all that I am
runs through my fingers
like water
from another source
To watch
and to feel
and to know
the end
as it approaches
l'at, l'at? (slowly, slowly?)
in the measured movements of
your body
in the lines of your face
in the grip of your hands
in your dark eyes
brimming with
bewilderment
questions
accusations against God
and tears
Your tears

Hilda Schiff

THE TABLECLOTH

These things you touch
I handle every day.

Here is the tablecloth
You hemmed for frequent use
Initialled casually in
Red and white, not expertly
But in a homespun way,
The task of a wet afternoon,
Your children playing at your side
Or at a little distance in a further room,
The clock's small ticking while you sew,
Still softly clicking.

Still time before you need to
Stir, before the knives and forks
We use for best these days
Need leave their drawer,
Laid out for supper or for tea.
Still time before
That brutal butt came down
And sealed you in the wagon
Bound for death, the clock
So soon to cease its ticking.

Your hands touch this
As mine do now.
But I am at a loss
To grasp the meaning of
This link beyond the grave,
(What link? What grave?)

Or look up at the face of God
Who let it happen.

Myra Schneider

ROOT VEGETABLE STEW

When dark nights eat up afternoons
I sweat onions in sunflower oil,
weigh out carrots, a swede,
and tapering baby parsnips
with old-age skins on flesh
that fattened underneath the light
in a cradling of clay, grit, stones.

I take the swede, a misshapen globe
marred with scars, cut it in two.
The apricot bulk makes my head
hum with summer. I slice up
the snow-white parsnips, then tip
lentils, seeds of a butterfly-
petalled plant, into the pan.

Opening the door to throw the peelings
in a pail, I bump into snouting cold.
It smells of woodsmoke, bites
as I stare at the park bristled
with black. Frost is stiffening leaves,
grasses, and I feel myself woven
to this land's Saxon past when winter

was a giant who trampled crops in fields,
snuffed breath with icicle fingers -
though this was not the country
of my forbears, though rootlessness
was a wound I bore till turned thirty,
I was warmed enough by love
to put down roots in myself.

When chill sinks its teeth in my ribs,
I retreat to the stove, dip a spoon.
The heat-swollen lentils are melting
among the hulking vegetables,
and yellowbrown as November woods.
I add lemon and fried spices,
stir them in, ladle the stew.

THE MATCH FACTORY IN BETHNAL GREEN

Three ladies sat in the velvet shade
of a mulberry tree, away from the heat
and dusty clop where I stood staring
at their shining windows, at the lace curtains
that took my fancy, at the garden green
with grass that wouldn't grow in my black yard.

In my sweaty pinafore I looked at lupins,
at white-mice fingers busy stitching,
at faces smooth as porcelain, thought
of taffeta scraps I'd sewn, wishing
and wishing for a doll to clothe. "Grubby..."
a voice slapped. Ashamed, I ran.

By the stables: the smell of timber, the rasp
of sawing. Not a single drop of shadow
as I queued with the matchbox makers, longing
to play on earth as clean as the ground
where three ladies skilled with needles,
sat in the shade of the mulberry tree.

Beyond the stinking privy by my fence:
crowds of flies on cows standing
neck to neck in mud and dung.
My mouth trembled as I mumbled to a man
with a scab-red face but no pennies
were handed out - not enough boxes done.

No dinner of mash or faggots. My stomach
rumbled; I all but snivelled. A smell
of roasting beef flowed from the kitchen
as I caught the gleam of copper pans.
A door unfastened, revealed a maid
in the stiff snow of cap and apron.

Behind the mansion I stood with children
in skimpy bodies and women yoked
to sad faces, some with little clothing
and scarcely any boots to their feet.
At the front: three ladies with fancywork,
cooled under a lattice of mulberry leaves.

NEED

a postcard of 'Mother and Daughter' by Schiele

The mother is small-boned,
delicate as a folded bird.
Her long flamingo-red
off-the-shoulder gown
exposes the sad slant of her neck.

178

The daughter has not thought
to hide her nakedness: tight
twin buds of buttocks,
a narrow trunk. Impulsively
she hugs the quiet fire that wraps

her mother. Their heads touch,
mingle haystack-gold hair
threading from the same source.
Here is closeness beyond flesh -
each comforting, comforted.

The tenderness stops my breath
with a blade of pain that splits me
apart. In the gape is my mother's face
closed to mine, the silence
dividing us cold as glass.

And down a passage I make out
a dark-haired child - not me
but her. Blanks for eyes she shrinks
from the woman whose pecking mouth
never sweetens with kisses.

In pale outline behind
the bitter woman is a girl
whose fingers flutter music. Duty
chains her to sickroom, kitchen,
rubs salt into her feelings...

So it goes back, must not go on.
I sift feathers of kindness, find
illuminating words, fill myself;
mark the place in my book
with the clasped mother and daughter.

CROSSING POINT

In memory of Paula Schneider

Everything was new:
her coat heavy as winter;
the boys' short trousers;
their shoes shining like ice.

Everything was new. The train
had wrenched her from Vienna -
Raindorfgasse that still held
the sheen of her childhood;
from loved faces with hope
bandaged tightly over worry,
from the thin waving of hands.

The station at Emmerich was new too:
concrete pillars straddling arches;
platforms spotless as German Maidens;
the strut of uniformed legs.

The red J stamped
in the corner of her passport
branded her cheeks long before
the compartment door was opened.

'You and your two children step down.'
The air smelt of fear
and as the train moved on,
the few miles to Holland
became infinity.

Her knees threatened to unhinge
when the boys were prised
out of her sight to be searched.
The control she'd built for months,
queuing to beg permits from clerks
ungiving as grilles, collapsed.

'Don't take them!' She sobbed.
Didn't see the unmalicious,
bovine eyes, the boots hoofing
in embarrassment. In her bag
one set of papers was out of date.
In her head the Fuehrer's words
fired and fired.

A woman checked the body
inside her coat, unlaced
her shoes. She was held
in a cold swing of terror.

The children returned intact.

It was dark when the train
pulled out. passed rows
of windows dimmed for war.
She knew they'd crossed
the border when light splashed
from every farm. Relief swept
like sun over greening fields
fenceless to the sky.

Valerie Sinason

CORSETS LIKE PEACH WHALES

Here they come again
the babushkas
with their swollen pat-a-cake arms
and pogroms of pastry

Feeling the quality
of stained shirts, arranged marriages

They chop onions, liver, children

Corsets like peach whales
gobble the air round the streaked line

False teeth chatter curses
into empty beakers

Empty mouths wrinkle round
secrets of linament
and lavender water

Here they come again
cursing at me

with my Hampstead dress
and Petticoat Lane
and my voice of many colours

THE CRUCIBLE

I am the lily of the valley and the rose of Sharon
Lilith the woman walks with her wounds singing
a day to be alive on
a day for the God-dammed babies to cry for a tongue

She walks in the heat of His hatred
in the flames of His inquisition

The woman with the words singing inside her
how they call for homes and she has left them
the woman whose blood turned the crops sour
the woman whose heat warmed the old Adam's earth

Orphaned as the sky
She lives at the stake of His private hell
the gold chain around her neck like a noose

Lilith daughter of the goddess once sought justice
The father and the son
sent her to the devil

ENGLISH JEW ABROAD

(1)

I sit in my gold shawl
on the sunny side of the ship
the white cliffs of England melting away
soft as an icecream

183

Leaving
Once it was not as easy as this
Once it was hard just to come
yet here I am off to Paris
with the yellow badge
that never leaves me
blooming like a daffodil

(2)

On the Seine
the day after the bomb Goldenberg's
carved faces of saints and gargoyles
shining from the bridge
the old battle between good and evil

and on the quayside
"mort aux juifs"

Portraits in Montmartre
the stroll down the Champs D'Elysee
and *Juifs Dehors* on the shutters of the Tabac
and *Mort L'Israel* on the metro
at the Place de la Bastille-
the only graffiti

The world drains to a yellow badge

(3)

But *"Fermé"* says the woman curtly
when asked for *"The Times"*
though clearly open for *"Le Figaro"*
Anti-English, an ironic treat

And at the terminal
queuing as only the English queue
hearing the sounds of Birmingham,
Yorkshire, London
Suddenly I am English again
and though I think of you my grandparents
cold from Odessa pogroms to meet the London rain

Today as I sail in
I am London as the ta ra ra waves
London as jellied eels
and my yellow badge grins like a fried egg

PASSOVER

You are still leaving Egypt
you are still driven out
insists the Haggadah

Wherever you are
thank the eternal one
and say next year in Jerusalem

Now I'm in West Hamstead
quite happily
and next year will be Cornwall
or Lido de Jesolo
not Jerusalem

But you still chase me
God of my fathers
with your "Hello stranger"
double binding oaths
and promises of plagues
to heathens and unbelieving children

185

What a way to make a family eat together

Curses, bitter herbs and chicken soup

Five thousand years of family dinners
with the empty chair for Elijah
who neatly stayed away

Anna Sotto

POEMS FOR KATIA

i) *Memento Mori*

Chatting over tea
in the ten o'clock break
as teachers do -
I catch a glimpse
of the blue number
tattooed on your arm.

I try to see you
as you were,
a shaven head
a nameless face,
reduced to
this number.

I want to speak out
and touch you
but...
we chat over tea
in the ten o'clock break
as teachers do.

v) *A 6893*

She didn't cry
when they removed
her clothes, her ring,
her shoes, her hair,
But when they took away
her name -
she wept.

KHAMSIN

The Khamsin blows
through shuttered eyes
of sleepy Safed...
velvet contentment
seeping through
dulling us
into one blank lull
of spaceless nought,
-the holy silence
of your embrace-
the khamsin blows
obliterating
threadbare words,
blunted swords - and us.

TO THE LILAC GIVER

Don't smother my grave
with armfuls of lilac,
bring one frail sprig
while I am alive.

Gloria Tessler

CHICKEN SOUP

Glycerine-limbed, koshered,
within your icy membrane
you curl reproachful fingers.
Your latter end the pot
and mine the worm,
you were
as unprepared for death as I.
These gnarled and knotted
fists of feet once strutted,
red-crested, fearing no evil.
Now your soup boileth over.
In the shrinkage of your dead flesh
I touch
your stiff, admonitory claw,
innocent, shaped from childhood;
yet to make soup out of you
who have barely lived out
your chicken days and now, in death
look scaly, speckled as
an old man's flesh, seems cruel.
I apologise
for my weakness, for the sin
I have committed
in eating and drinking.
Some crowing army awaits
as you lie
amid chopped carrots, onion and celery,
some archangel of chickenkind
smiles at the gates of Heaven.
My broken promises to you
are a flurry of feathers before Yom Kippur,
down the years of my childhood,

down the aeons of Jewish mothers
as your bird-blood flows
from Dachau to Disneyland.

BONE WOMAN

For Irma Kien and the Six Million

Bone woman,
I am woman of bone.
lone woman, my eyes are stone.
I break easily, small fissures
have marbled me like cracked china.
Do not expect me
to sing for Old Zion
under the sad willow.

The fossil-flesh recalls
its undulations
that moved men
and grew children.
Women of Israel,
I take the measure
of your acanthine flesh;
on its spikes I have grown my soul.

I am your Auschwitz skeleton.
Lipless, I grin beside rows of spectacles,
that catch the light like dull students,
And I wonder if they see me,
those people with their Rolex watches
and Nikon cameras.

Can you see my doll eyes,
dark as agate, my toe joints adangle?
They blink for the photos, they cannot help it,
for here are cyanide canisters,
and there, the serpent coils of human hair.
The visitors blink and smile at the future.

At Auschwitz the clocks have stopped
in the clutch of the dark season.
they have airlocked time so that I may move free
within my winter. My eagle flight
has landed; I touch base in ice wadis
that will not thaw.

Yet to amuse you I would wear
a lampshade on my head
and dance for the festivals,
as we did, when we threw sweets to children

just for the joy of watching them run,
for the joy of knowing the flesh of their laughter.

If I could feel, I would dance now,
a rich dance in a place of privilege;
undulating; veiled I would go, like a harem girl,
dipping into her erotic memory.
And with stamping feet
I would slide the earth back under the sky.

MISCARRIAGE

Your body came to me
twisted in a coil of blood.
But, bodiless, I knew you,
your nature rooted
in the chocolate nights
where we celebrate children.
Now your empty birth
has filled me.
Knowledge of you
binds me to your not-quite-being.
Vacuumed and flushed clean,
they sweep me to another ward,
etherised from the safe-delivered.
Their cries, fallen to the earth's threshing floor,
to me are shards, life-shavings,
while I sensed what cannot be encompassed,
and mourn the never-known
and ever, ever-to-be.

Leah Thorn

HOLOCAUST JUNKIE

I'm a Holocaust junkie
and I need my fix

Can't get no high
won't get no kicks

till I hear those stories
till I see those pics

Gimme gimme horror
gimme gimme gore

emaciated bodies
piles galore
stripey pajamas
and eyes that implore

Gimme gimme terror
gimme gimme more
gimme gimme more
gimme gimme MORE!

I want to feel something
I need to heal
It's the best I know
it's the smartest deal

Will somebody listen
while I cry my pain?
Will somebody hold me
as the terror reigns?

because
I can't move
I can't think
I can't trust
I can't blink

when the terror gets me
I blow a fuse
It doesn't make sense what they did to the jews

so I read the books
and I see the films
no rest there
so I sit and stare
eyes go blank
body slumps
relive the horrors
and I'm in the dumps

I'm a Holocaust junkie
need someone to say sorry
won't you please say sorry
just say you're sorry.

I'm a Holocaust junkie
I am sharp
I am hard
Nothing gets me
cos I'm on my guard

I wear only black
and I crop my hair
monochrome resistance
to the rage I fear

Keep it all in
Keep it all down
Rage that engulfs
Feel it and I'll drown

Gimme gimme horror
gimme gimme screams
night after night of violent dreams

Gimme gimme terror
gimme extremes
gimme extremes
gimme EXTREMES

I wanna be through this
I want my life
I wanna know I'm perfect
and deserve no strife.

I wanna be cradled
with nothing to lose
to trust and to love
whoever I choose
to trust and to love
whoever I choose

I'm a Holocaust junkie
See I'm alive
Even if they didn't
I know I survived

In honour or them
I live my life
Live my life
Live my life
for me

THIS ONE IS, I THINK, TO BE KNOWN

I can't do this she says
I don't do this she says
Then she does

No, I don't dance she says
I only look like a dancer she says
Then she dances

And the body stretches
and fills space
that is hers
that she thought she could never have again
and she sees
there is no straitjacket
only the tightness of self-criticism
and the constant searching for the criticism of others
to prove

I can't do this
I don't do this
And then she does

She has
photos
of her back
back-lit at her waist
hips rounded and ready for sweeping hands
She has flesh

As her hair grows
she leaves the Holocaust behind
forever

I can't she says
I don't she says
Yet she does

She falls back into water
Leans against unseen energies
Allows unknown hands to rest on her
Hears the story of Abraham and Isaac
and knows

I can't trust she says
I don't trust she says
Then she does
Life was never meant to be like this she says
I wasn't supposed to be close to you she says
I can't love she says
I don't love she says

And she does

Theresa Turk

THE LAST SYNAGOGUE IN RHODES

Lucia, show me your hand
with the numerals
tattooed on the back of the wrist

Draw the blue curtains with the
gold lions rampant.
Inside the ark are mantled scrolls

with crowns and finials shaped
like pomegranates,
hung with their silent silver bells.

Come, let us stand under the
open portico
clasped by the winter's leafless vine.

Your Rhodian patronym,
Modiano, is
incised on a marble tablet.

What of the hundred others?
They left their ashes
far away in the cold Slav earth.

Your feet slip on the moving
sands of history.
You have become the very stuff

of academic theses,
the solitary
relic of two millennia.

When you die this place becomes
a monument that
crumbles without a caretaker.

Then there will be only the
antiquarian
to know and touch these ancient stones.

LETTER TO MARC CHAGALL

Dear Marc Chagall,
did you know, your horizontal rabbi in the sky,
he was Shlomo the Schvartser,
my great, great, grandfather?
Pallid, squint-eyed,
night after night
he grappled with the blurred dagesh,
in shuttered rooms,
by the dim circle
of the half groschen candle stump.

The admonition of the young
his speciality; author of tracts concerning disobedience.
I have inside me his bequest.
It stirs still in the marrow of my bones,
I see it in each censuring fore finger,
the words, "Thou shalt not",
trouble my wakeful nights.

He knew it too-
that wildest, youngest son -
wrong to have named him Absolom.
On that, his last Shabbat,
he took his leave of innocence,
exultant, tore out the pages from the books,
the harvest chaff of the long nights,
flung up a thousand yellow flakes
and made a snow storm in the summer sky.

And the Almighty, blessed be his name,
mirthful at pride brought low,
bellowed out mighty gusts, shook the globe,
filled the greened caftan folds,
lifted the black bat Shlomo to the stars.

Marc Chagall, it was in a dream,
between two heart beats,
that you saw Shlomo,
face plaster white,
brows black as hell,
aloft in your painted heaven.

ANSWERS

I never forgot how it was the first time.
Your face was puffy and red and lost.
I knew you had something, something bad
to tell me. "What's wrong?", I asked,
but "dead" was one of those words
you never could say out loud.
"It's the Booba - she's ill, so ill"
and tears that were big and very terrible
spilled down your cheeks.

I wrote, on the back of a used envelope,
"Don't cry - she will get better",
and pushed the torn blue scrap to you over the table -
"No, she won't get better - ever", you replied
and you explained to me about the mirrors covered
with pillow cases and the little stools.
For a year after that, every Saturday morning
you took me with you to Shul -
"She would have wanted me to say Kaddish"-
but we hardly went again after that -
"None of it matters any more", you said.

The next time, with Mother, it was different.
The words you couldn't say were the name
of the illness and the machine that
kept her breathing and which had
to be switched off in the end.
At the cemetery you were
so choked you could hardly get through
the prayer for the dead - but you knew it by heart.
The Rabbi frowned
when you said this time there would be no Shiva;
that you could mourn without help.
When we got back and I opened the dressing table
drawers and found the rouge box and the shiny blue
flask of "Evening in Paris", I remembered
the torn envelope. "When I die", you said,
"please, no Shiva. None of it
means anything". But your face softened when
you found the eggs. "You must eat something",
you whispered and you boiled them hard - two each.

That last time, when you never answered the 'phone,
I found you lying by the high, red
mahogany bed - it had held life
for me - and now death for you.
Men, for whom no mystery remains,

with blank faces and deft hands,
they come for you. "I wish you long life.
His Hebrew name? His tallis - if you don't mind".
They said the words.
And under the velvet bag, there were the
photographs - sepia and soft.
The Booba and the Zeyde, who looked like the last Czar,
my mother, long plaits, when she first came to England,
me - defiant, square, in that first gym slip,
and you - the A.R.P. Warden - with men whose faces
smile from archive libraries.
Oh, my sons, oh, my sons, you do not know
of low stools or dark blue velvet bags,
but you will know the emptiness they filled.

Michelene Wandor

EVE TO LILITH

don't get me wrong -
I have nothing against
first wives

ok, so you laid him
first; that's merely
a fact of life
so you got to know
all his little habits, like
picking his nose
when he reads in bed

he didn't do that with you?
I see

I'm not jealous. I don't
believe in jealousy, and
what I don't believe in
doesn't hurt me. But tell me
honestly, what did you do to the poor man?
He's a nervous wreck.
He can't stand up to his boss, he has
pains in his side all the time -
I mean, something must have happened
to leave a man
so scarred.

He told me how beautiful you were.
The dark, dramatic type.

Usually he doesn't talk about you
but when we - well, long ago -
when - at night -
we - in the dark, always -
he used to call your name
at a certain moment.

It's none of my business
but you must have done
something very special
to make a man
remember you so

LILITH TO EVE

I merely said 'no'.

That's when he gave me
his attention
for the first time

LILITH'S DANCE

Lilith sins?

Lilith sings
Lilith speaks many a cross word
Lilith has an anger like love
like a procession of pillars
of fire
Lilith has the delight
of a woman scorned

he modelled me
I was his clay thing
into me he breathed life
I became his *golem*
I went forth and I destroyed
havoc my middle name

I am the *dybbuk* of delight
I slip into the souls
of those who need me

perhaps you breathed
just a little
too much life, a sniffle too long
but once tasting the air
I would not be still, not
be silent, not return
to my feet of clay

I will not gather dust
I do not cower beneath cobwebs
I do not fear the hot streets
I walk
in the middle
of the pavement

I do not hug the shade
of cowardly buildings
I do not stay in my ghetto
but I strut and stride
into the ghetto
of men
I interrupt
the invisible universal
which denies men their souls
and women their being

I do not creep

I do not crawl

see

I am proud

I have taken the cloth
from my mirror
of mourning

for your birthday
(if gods have birthdays)
I shall give you
a mirror

SOME INVITATIONS

Jael is carving me a long table

Deborah has promised not to pass judgement
on the dinner, unless it's praise

Delilah is planning to dye her
hair green, to go
with the new curtains
and the tree

Ruth and Naomi are bringing
a double sleeping-bag

Pope Joan can leave the baby
in my bedroom; Solomon's
two lady friends are bringing
their babies too
Perseus and Peter Pan will
amuse the children with flying tricks

the Queen of Sheba is dropping
in after dinner
for a cognac

Jezebel can leave the dogs outside

Esther and Vashti will bring the
book they are writing together, and
doubtless argue all the way
through dinner

Persephone is bringing her mother;
they can sit opposite one another

Medusa and her Gorgon sisters
are going to play a trio for recorders
Andromeda is bringing some seaweed,
chinese-style-fried

Baba Yaga and Sarah are both
bringing chicken soup

Wendy is just going
to enjoy herself
for a change

and that nice girl Judy, from
Chicago, who is very fond of
dinner parties,
is coming

that's a lot of guests; a lot
of *kneidlach*

EVE TAKES A TRIP

the soup's on a low flame
clean socks and shirts
in the cupboard

I breathed polish on the candlesticks
I dusted the incense

butter's in the freezer
chopped liver in the
pottery dish covered with cling-film

all you need to buy
each day
is bread and fruit

the biscuit tin is full
and there's a new
packet of *matzo*
on the top shelf

I'm taking some ham
and pickle sandwiches
on rye

expect me when you see me.

Lyn Westerman

VIXEN

I slink along your street at night,
to sniff for scraps you may have left
for someone else, perhaps.
Cling to walls and hedges
and shrink on outer fringes
of other peoples lives;
trusting the dark to mask my shape
or my identity.

Watchful, wary, I sense
the presence of approaching menace;
hear men's beat of feet
and freeze before they reach
where I am blended in.
Then flee.

Each night I do the same,
pulled by the pain
my hunger for you brings.
Tonight there will be no feasting.
I will lie awake till dawn
and gnaw on bones of broken dreams.

JEWISH CEMETERY AT BUSHEY

The houses of the dead
stare whitely to the East;
towards Jerusalem.

I think about them
as I queue
impatiently in Safeways.

Shopping for eternity
as the years shuffle forward
one by one.

Side by side
never touching
the same mask worn by each.

Do they see us
as we bustle by them,
chasing time
as it chases us?

The white stones gleam like smiles.

WITHOUT A SAFETY NET

Far above the bubble-bath faces
I swing from flashing silver
uncurling into the air, gripped
by the cling of my skin,
ankle coupling on steel,
slide to a high of blue spangles and boa
then shed the feathers to the hungry-mouthed.

I mouth on gold,
spinning to a fishnet shroud,
tethered to the sky-grimed ceiling.

Feeling my legs again
around the dancing bar
I hook into atmosphere
reaching further, further.

Now it is only me,
the thrum of breaths
rising like the drumming
of beats which catch
on a slack stillness,
the shape waiting in the shadows
or empty as a trick of light.

I open my arms
and
fling
myself
into
the
dark

Julie Whitby

THE VIOLET ROOM

The violet room, they called it,
yet we knew otherwise.

Misty, violet curtains hung there:
moistly welcoming, oh yes.

But through their careful lies,
we sensed its sumptuous secrets,

judged them dear as wild strawberries,
lay in wait for lurid hints:

an uncut novel in French
scrumptiously virginal –

and smelling superb to us
as croissants and coffee.

The aroma of tobacco,
not papa's surely?

A drawer crackling with lace petticoats,
unworn. Why? What for?

Our days had a point, a purpose,
we waited, bided our time.

But nothing decisive
was ever discovered.

We consoled ourselves finally
with Enid Blyton, Jane Austen. Or, unabashed,

tried on Mamma's lipstick
in the dusty mirror of that ghosted room.

At other times wept copiously,
without knowing why, hollow as our dolls.

The violet room we call it now,
yet they know otherwise.

ICON

It doesn't even smell of you: ochre
with dirt, musty, lacking your especial smell,
warm, sweet. Why choose so mediocre
an icon? Why clutch it then? Hard to tell.
The moon's immaculate medal: yellow and cream,
is pinned to the sky as if to a soldier's murky battle-dress,
yet still how fitting an image of love's dream
it remains, as voluptuous trees whisper their caress.
But this indifferent garment (always here
under my pillow), its everydayness, flimsy
pathos reassures, brings you near.
Stained, changed by time- as you are- not whimsy
but wart-embracing love, makes me treasure this best
of all gifts, my companion in absence: your vest.

Tamar Yoseloff

LIMPETS

My mother still tells me about the day
on Avon Beach when I brought a jellyfish
laced with blue and red veins, live wires,
through the throngs of screaming mothers
and unbelieving children to present her
with my treasure. It didn't sting me,
I've always been lucky like that.

Now you show me the limpets clinging
to their stability, a rock in high tide
that will be drowned. You tell me
how each one digs a groove that fits
like a glove, knows home by its contours.
But if they are prised from their place,
they can't go back, and they die.

Each day I pass the woman who lives
outside the bankrupt travel agent.
I pretend I don't notice, but I know
she watches me, her eyes burn with secrets.
She drinks McDonalds coffee from
a styrofoam cup, keeps her umbrella open,
speaks to the pigeons in lowered tones.

The night I brought you home we made love
quietly, to pacify the neighbours.
Billie Holiday whispered from a dark
corner of the room, candles cast our
shadows larger than life. We talked
for hours about serial killers, riots,
the general state of affairs. After,

we lay like the limpets, your body
a shell for mine, safe on our rocky place,
as the rain poured down outside.

THE JEWISH GHETTO IN VENICE

My mother, as always, sensibly attired
in a pleated skirt, flat-heeled shoes.
I stand a head taller, the holes in my jeans
made cleanly with a knife, a man's jacket
which hung to my knees. The only holiday
we ever spent together alone, the photo taken
by the owner of the *pensione* the day the U.S.
bombed Libya. *Your President Reagan is a good man,*
he had told us, holding up an Italian paper.

We arrived in the midst of a garbage strike,
the tourists frightened off. Around every corner
that smell greeted us like a guide,
as we searched for landmarks, a sign that we were
not lost. We found the synagogue as the light
was fading, took refuge in its musty hall,
the scent of polished wood. The light edged
through the high windows, patterning the floor.

We may have been closest then, just before
I began my grown up life; it was never mentioned.
in retrospect, simply a holiday without my father,
who would have checked us into the best hotel,
made reservations in the grand dining room
full of stately old-school Americans, unaffected
by world events. Instead we walked slowly
through sombre alleyways and courtyards,
finding places left unmarked on the map.

Barbara A Zanditon

I GO OUT OF MY WAY TO HAND LOST ARTICLES IN TO THE POLICE

At the theatre I surrender buttons.
"Here," I say pressing them into the palms of
a startled usherette.
"Somebody lost these."
I try hard to please.

I help old people across the street.
Startle the blind with unwelcome assistance at lights.
But I pass by the homeless.

I love collecting-boxes. Any opportunity to give.
"Here," I say, stuffing the pennies and pound coins
into slots for Bosnia, syphilis, heart disease.
But I walk past the old man who is homeless
with his thin blanket and fleas.
I plead poverty, unknowingness.

I help mothers with pushchairs
up and down stairs. Greet every opportunity
to be kind but I put the homeless
out of mind. They might speak to me.

I like life sanitised: clean giving -
the dead or the dying but not this living rebuke.
I know their condition is outrageous.
Someone should help them,
but they might be contagious:

The man who lives
in High Holborn -
who, now as the evenings get light
sits bolt upright
staring at us as we rush past
his head and shoulders
rising above the clean cardboard of his box.

And the mad woman
with her rags
and dirt
and bags.

And the young man with the sign:
"I am hungry
I am homeless."
And unspoken:
"Please be kind."

And the shrewd look
in the beggar's eyes
sizing me up as I walk by.

ON VIEWING A POSTCARD REPRODUCTION
OF A PAINTING OF A NUDE BY LUCIAN FREUD

The woman displayed
like a carcass
across the couch.

Legs splayed.
Head flung backward.
She is green and drained of blood.

Humans require love.
Frequently do not receive it.

Did God watch as she was painted
stroke by stroke?

And who rubbed her ankles
or touched her sore shoulders?
And did she drink tea?
And how did she feel
splayed like a carcass?
Her pubic hair forever there
on the canvas for anyone to touch.
Her legs bent back at the knees
and slightly parted.
Her private parts almost
accessible.

Was she cold?
Did she feel exposed?
And after?

Was it an honour to be painted?
Did she feel loved?

I WILL POT MY LOVE LIKE A HYACINTH

In a blue bowl the bulb
exposed
the green leaf tipped through earth.

In a blue bowl the bulb unfolds
the leaf pulled back
and buds.
Blue flowers
grouped on a single stalk
and bursting.
Petals curled out and overlap
exposing each centre
revealing a scent so rich and sweet
it sticks to me coating the lining of my throat.

I will pot my love like a hyacinth
in a blue bowl.
Let me water and tend
he will root and grow
pushing out green shoots
&
blooming in a tenderness of love
come Spring.

THE CONTRIBUTORS

Sigrid Agocsi was born in Munster in 1961 and is a performer and theatre director. She founded the Munich Institute for Acting, Singing, Speech and Voice Therapy. She followed her husband, the composer and classical guitarist Janos Agocsi, to London, and is now mainly living there where she also works as a stage- and film-coach and talent finder for the music industry.

Liane Aukin has lived all her life in North London. Her plays Beowulf and On Top were both performed at the Theatre Upstairs and Silver Lady at Birmingham Rep. She writes for radio and television and is currently completing a Screen One for BBC TV. Her dramatisation of Woolfs' Between the Acts won a Sony Award and The Mushroom Picker was nominated best TV serial 1993.

Joan Ballin was educated at the Universities of North Wales and Leeds. She taught English in a Sheffield comprehensive school but for many years now has taught sick children in hospital and at home. She has had other single poems published and is working on her first collection.

Wanda Barford has written extensively on the experience of being a Jew in the twentieth century. In a collection, Sweet Wine and Bitter Herbs, due out from Flambard in 1996, she deals not only with the deportation of members of her family to Auschwitz, but also with the sense of loss, dislocation and strangeness experienced by people moving across the world in search of safety.

Janet Berenson-Perkins is an American who has lived in London for over 20 years. She is a professional Jewish educator, working for Finchley Reform Synagogue and the Centre for Jewish Education. She also teaches meditation, Women's Torah study and creative spirituality. Janet is part of Belladonna Women's Theatre Group and directs New Connections. Married with two daughters, she has been writing poetry all her life.

Julie Bernstein was born in London in 1971, but was brought up in Kent. Her father was brought up Jewish, but married outside the religion. Julie graduated last year with a B.A. (Hons) in Drama and Experience of Writing and lives in Derby.

Nadine Brummer was born and brought up in Manchester and is of East European immigrant stock. She has been a psychiatric social worker and a lecturer at Goldsmiths' College. She began writing late, and has had poems published in magazines and anthologies, including New Poetry 4 (Arts Council/P.E.N.), Writing Women and Rialto.

Liz Cashdan says she couldn't be a writer without also being a daughter (ex), sister, mother, grandmother, wife (ex), cousin, aunt and friend. She describes herself as a walker/traveller in space and time, a teacher/lecturer in schools and universities who encourages other people to write. Alongside these, she is a Jew and a socialist. Her latest collection of poetry is Laughing All the Way, published by Five Leaves Publications.

Norma Cohen works as an actress and writes on dance for the TES. Writing includes Theatre Works: A Guide to Working in the Theatre (National Theatre/Theatre Museum), chapters in Out of Focus (Women's Press) and Death of a Mother: Daughters' Stories (Harper Collins). Her plays include Who Cares? and She Who Has Dreamed. Norma has also written comic monologues and a short story The Last Supper for radio. She has a sixteen year-old daughter.

Tricia Corob has had poetry, articles and reviews published in a variety of magazines and anthologies. She teaches theatre studies for Birkbeck College and works as a counsellor specializing in issues of spirituality and creativity.

Lynette Ellen Craig was born in Birmingham in 1949, but found her spiritual home in N.W. London. She is married with three children. Her poetry has been published in anthologies and magazines, her New Year's resolution is to write more. Lynette sings in choirs, and loves theatre, especially Shakespeare.

Iona Doniach was born in London in 1938. Her mother and grandparents were all known artists, her father's side being teachers, linguists and scholars. She studied painting at the Royal College of Art and has had numerous exhibitions. Iona now teaches in a large comprehensive school in Coventry and writes and illustrates allegorical stories for children.

Jane Dorner is a non-fiction writer who has published 14 books including an anthology of children's poetry, three books on fashion and a handbook for writers using new technology. She has had a long career in publishing including being an editor at Longman, an art editor at Weidenfeld and Nicolson and a fiction reader for Penguin. Jane now works freelance as a writer and editor, turning to poetry in moments of emotional crisis.

Ruth Fainlight was born in New York City but has lived in England since the age of 15. She has published nine collections of poems, her Selected Poems appearing earlier this year. She has also published two collections of short stories and written opera libretti. Her poems have been translated into French, Portuguese and Hebrew.

Rachel Castell Farhi was born in London in 1965 into a mixed heritage - a Sephardi mother from Jerusalem and an

Anglo-Irish father. This dual identity informs her writing. After university and qualifying in teaching she worked in Israel, meeting and marrying Oded. They have a daughter, Naomi. Rachel works in special needs education but also freelances as a journalist.

Elaine Feinstein is a poet and novelist and was made a Fellow of the Royal Society of Literature in 1980. She received a Cholmondeley Award for her poetry in 1990, and in the same year, an Honorary D. Lit. from the University of Leicester. Her Selected Poems was published by Carcanet last year.

Thilde Fox was born in Vienna in 1930, coming to England with the Kindertransport in 1938 and lived with the Barnett family in Hull. In 1953 she moved to Israel. She has an MA in English Literature from Haifa University, where she has been a teacher trainer and lecturer. Thilde has also taught English in High School. She is married with three children, one daughter-in-law and four grandchildren.

Berta Freistadt is a poet, playwright and story teller. her publishers include Virago, Women's Press, Oscars Press, Methuen and Stride. She is a Londoner, a patrilineal Jew, a gardener, a cat owner and a member of Beit Klal Yisrael. She likes TV, the tarot, food, sleep, friends, sex and shopping. And getting published!

Adèle Geras was born in Jerusalem in 1944 and lives in Manchester. More than forty of her books for children and young adults have been published, and a collection of poetry called Voices from the Doll's House from Rockingham Press.

Miriam Halahmy is a North London poet and a member of the Highgate Poetry Society. Her poetry has been published in a wide range of magazines and her first collection, Stir Crazy, was published last year by Hub Editions. Miriam is also a reviewer and has recently completed a novel set in modern Israel.

Joyce Herbert's poetry has been appearing in the Jewish Quarterly since 1980. Her work has also appeared in Poetry Review, New Poetry, Poetry Wales, Poetry Ireland Review and Stand. Poetry Wales have published a collection of her work. Joyce read English at University College Cardiff and lives in South Glamorgan.

Nini Herman was born Nini Ettlinger in Berlin in 1925, leaving for Britain in 1938. After qualifying as a doctor she worked as a family doctor in London and Suffolk for 25 years before training to be a psychoanalytical psychotherapist. Currently living in West Kensington Nini is married to the artist Josef Herman, whose biography she is writing, to be published by Quartet. She has four children and has written five books including My Kleinian Home.

Tamar Hodes was born in Israel and lived in Greece and South Africa before settling in London in 1967. She read English and Education at Cambridge and has since taught adults and children, also working for the BBC and writing poetry and prose. She was one of Virago's New Poets in 1993. Tamar is married with two children and lives in Staffordshire. Her hobbies include overdosing on gefilte fish and being in her pyjamas by 8.30 pm.

Sue Hubbard is a poet and art critic. She writes for Time Out and the New Statesman and broadcasts on Kaleidoscope. A founder member of The Blue Nose Poets she has published two poetry pamphlets and Enitharmon have brought out a full-length collection, Everything Begins With the Skin. She is at present doing an MA at the University of East Anglia.

Judith Issroff is a South African born British-Israeli. She is a psychiatrist and psychoanalyst and founder-director of the Israeli Association for Social Change and Solution of Conflicts. Judith is a pessimist who operates optimistically, a good liver and loves forests, cooking, painting, music, art, movement and playing with words.

Shirley Jaffe
Born Wembley - moved seaside
Then London - Blitz!
Henrietta Barnett School - stagestruck!
Trained central - bliss!

Rep, panto, then Scarborough,
First Theatre-in-the-Round - heaven!
Married Tony, had Devora,
Then David. After seven

Years, films, radio, TV,
Emergency Ward Ten,
Directed amateurs, became Counsellor,
Drama Therapist, and then

Taught Blind School, Assertion Training,
Exiled Dorset, Murder Mystery -
Became Grandma, started writing
Won Blaxland Press Prize - (that's 60!)

Rebecca Jerrison (née Cowan) wrote Translating the Practice which was written following a meditation retreat last year. She says "It symbolises a time of personal transformation and hope for the future. I am not an established poet or writer, but like to use words to complement my art and drawing. I am strengthened to be part of a book celebrating the creativity of Jewish women. Shalom."

Stella Jones was born in 1948. She writes "I first wrote poems from boredom during A-level English. I continued when desperate in my then relationship after discovering Erica Jong and Streisand's 'Woman in Love'. I owe a lot to my mother and to the memories of Booba and Zeida who loved me and left me proud to stand up and be counted."

Dorothy Judd was born in South Africa and came to Britain aged 11. She took her first degree in Fine Art and trained as an Art Therapist, then as a psychoanalytical Child Psychotherapist, later specialising in working with terminal illness. Her first book, Give Sorrow Words - Working with a Dying Child was re-issued in a new expanded edition this year by Whurr. Dorothy is a Marital Psychotherapist and Clinical Lecturer at the Tavistock Centre. She is married with four children.

Lila Julius was born and educated in Toronto, and moved to Israel with her family in 1972. Her poetry, fiction and non-fiction have appeared in Canada, the United States, Great Britain, Australia and Israel. She lives on a farm in the Lower Galilee where she teaches courses and gives workshops in creative writing.

Lotte Kramer was born in Mainz and came to England in 1939 as a child refugee, her family were lost in the Holocaust. She did all kinds of work while studying Art and Art History at Richmond Institute. She began to write in 1970 and is widely published in magazines, anthologies and papers both in England and abroad and her poetry has been broadcast on television and radio. The Desecration of Trees and Earthquake and Other Poems are the latest of her six books.

Jane Liddell-King was born in London in 1947 and educated at South Hampstead High School and Girton College, Cambridge. She is the married mother of two daughters and five sons. After spending years teaching English and French she is now looking forward to the late completion of two books on women and education, Clever Girls and Girl 2000 for Fouth Estate.

Sonja Lyndon writes plays for radio and stage and is currently playwright-in-residence at South Hill Park Arts Centre. Her most recent play, The Strange Passenger, set in Terezin Ghetto, opens in London concurrently with the publication of this anthology. Sonja also writes short stories and is on the editorial board of Jewish Quarterly. She is the daughter of German refugee parents and she lives in North London where she was brought up on the borders of "Finchley Strasse". She enjoys three grown-up children, two sons and a daughter.

Rochelle Mass moved with her family in 1973, from Vancouver, to Beit HaShita, a kibbutz in Israel. She writes "My world includes the specifics of the dry, complex land that is now my home with the calm beauty of the Canadian landscape where I was born. I combine these geographical and spiritual addresses in my writing."

Gerda Mayer was born in Karlsbad and came to England in 1939 at the age of eleven. Among her collections are Treble Poets 2 (Elon, Halpern and Mayer) and The Knockabout Show, both from Chatto; Monkey on the Analyst's Couch, from Ceolfrith - a Poetry Book Society Recommendation - and A Heartache of Grass, from Peterloo.

Pamela Melnikoff was born in London and educated at North London Collegiate School. Pamela is the film critic of the Jewish Chronicle and author of three historical novels for children; The Star and the Sword, Plots and Players and Prisoner in Time, as well as a prize-winning children's play, The Ransomed Menorah, and the libretto of a cantata, Heritage, with music by Cyril Ornadel.

Joan Michelson is an American who lectures in English at the University of Wolverhampton. Her publications include fiction in New Writing 4 (Vintage), New Writing 3 (Minerva), Stand, Spare Rib, a chapter in Teaching Creative Writing (Open University), poetry in The Poetry Business Anthology and in In The Gold of the Flesh (Women's Press). She has one daughter.

Rena Minkoff is English by birth. Came to Israel with the Habonim movement in 1949. Some of her work has appeared in Arc, the journal of the Israeli Writers in English. Other items have appeared on the BBC World Service, in the Guardian and in Green's Magazine in the USA.

Lilian Mohin is a feminist, lesbian writer who believes in the revolutionary power of words. Born 1938 in Kent; grew up in the USA; lives and works (since 1970) in London. She's edited five anthologies (two of poetry, two of short stories, one forthcoming non-fiction) and enough other writers' work to slow the self which is a poet.

Cheryl Moskowitz was born in 1959 in Chicago and moved to England when she was eleven. As well as poetry, she has written plays and most recently her first novel. She also works as an actress and psychodynamic counsellor and lives in London with her husband Alastair, who is a musician, and their three children, Alice, George and Martha.

Danielle Nagler is 22 and a student at Clare College, Cambridge. She was educated at North London Collegiate School, where she wrote a play for the Lloyds Bank Young Theatre Challenge. Danielle has worked as a volunteer English teacher in Mexico and Bolivia. She plans a career in journalism and has contributed to the Glasgow Herald, The Independent and The Jewish Chronicle.

Linda Rose Parkes was born in 1951 in Jersey, Channel

Islands. She has an M.A. in creative writing from East Anglia University and worked in Adult Education and as a performance poet in Aachen for 16 years. She is now making her way back to London, to continue to teach and write. Her work has appeared in Rialto, Writing Women, Outposts, Wide Skirt, Oscars Press, Orbis, In The Gold of the Flesh, New Poets (Virago), As Girls Could Boast and Hen House Publications.

Sylvia Paskin lectures on Film and Television Studies and is particularly interested in the presentation of art and artists in the Media. She also lectures at the National Portrait Gallery on literary and cinematic subjects. Her work has appeared in the Guardian, The Monthly Film Bulletin, The Listener, New Statesman, Women's Review and various academic film books, and she is on the editorial board of the Jewish Quarterly. Sylvia is co-editor of Angels of Fire (Chatto) and Dancing the Tightrope (Women's Press).

Alix Pirani was born in London in 1929 and was educated at Cambridge. She has been an English teacher and lecturer for 25 years and since 1974 a practising psychotherapist. She leads workshops and seminars in Jewish and feminine spirituality and creativity. Her publications include The Absent Father: Crisis and Creativity and The Absent Mother: Restoring the Goddess to Judaism and Christianity. Alix has four children.

Anne Ranasinghe fled to England from Germany just before the start of the Second World War and is the only survivor of her family. Having become a nursing sister and gaining a Diploma in Journalism she married a Sinhalese Professor of the Colombo Medical Faculty and has lived in Sri Lanka for over 40 years. Anne has had eleven books published and has won the Sri Lankan Arts Council poetry prize twice.

Dr Azila Talit Reisenberger is an award winning writer who has had poetry and short stories published in many countries. Born in Israel, 1952. At present lives with husband Peter and 3 children in Cape Town, South Africa, where she lectures at the University. An active participant in the movement for women's equality in society, religion and the legal system.

Sibyl Ruth works for the Citizens Advice Bureau and is also a creative writing tutor with the Open College of the Arts. She lives in the West Midlands and her first poetry collection, Nothing Personal, was published by Iron Press in 1995.

Deborah Sacks graduated in English from New College, Oxford in 1993. She has assisted in writing an autobiography set during the period of the Russian Revolution. Her book reviews and articles have appeared in the Ham and High and the Times Literary Supplement. Poetry is her first love and she is currently working on a verse play on the Children's Crusade.

Eva Salzman was born in N.Y.C. and is now resident in the UK. Her work has appeared in the Times Literary Supplement, the Independent, the Observer, the New Yorker, Poetry Review and in Sixty Women Poets (Bloodaxe). She co-edits The Printer's Devil Magazine and is currently writer in residence at Springhill Prison in Buckinghamshire. The poems here are reprinted from The English Earthquake (Bloodaxe Books, 1992).

Elizabeth Sarah was born in 1955 and is a lesbian, a feminist, a writer and a rabbi. A graduate of LSE and Leo Baeck College, after five years' congregational work she is now one of the Directors of the Reform Movement in Britain. Elizabeth is a member of the Assembly of Rabbis' Executive and of the co-ordinating group of The Half Empty Bookcase - the Progressive Jewish Women's Studies Network. Her recent publications include The Biblical Account of the First Woman (in Women's Voices), Rabbi Regina Jones 1902-1944 and Beruria (in Hear Our Voice) and Judaism and Lesbianism (in Jewish Explorations of Sexuality).

Sue Sareen is a professional artist and illustrator based in Nottingham, the illustration on the cover of Dybbuk... is from her painting Sisters, depicting her mother and daughter. Sue's father was an assimilated Marxist Jew from Russia.

Hilda Schiff is a poet, short story writer and editor. She was educated at London and Oxford Universities. She is attached to Wolfson College, Oxford and is a freelance writer. Her publications include a collection of poems, A Condition of Being, Contemporary Approaches to English Studies and Holocaust Poetry. One of her poems forms part of the Reform Synagogues of GB's prayer-book.

Myra Schneider lives in North London and is a part-time teacher of adults with severely disabled adults. She is a compulsive writer. Her most recent poetry collections are Crossing Point (Littlewood) and Exits (Enitharmon). Her prose publications include novels for children and teenagers. Her poetry has appeared in many journals and anthologies and on Radio 4 and Radio 2.

Valerie Sinason is a Consultant Child Psychotherapist at the Tavistock Clinic and the Anna Freud centre, and Research Psychotherapist at St. George's Hospital Medical School. She is a columnist for the Guardian and her books include Mental Handicap and the Human Condition and Memory in Dispute (forthcoming).

Anna Sotto is a Scots/Jewish/Israeli and an EFL teacher

231

and writer. She says "I write textbooks for my pocket, unpublished novels for my mind and poetry for my soul".

Gloria Tessler is a London-born journalist/fiction writer. Her articles have appeared in national dailies, Sundays and the Jewish media; her short stories in British and European magazines and poems in various anthologies including Poetry Now! and A Woman's Place. She has completed her third novel and is beginning a biography. Married, with three children.

Leah Thorn is a performance poet, exploring issues of liberation through the spoken word. Both the selections here are taken from a performance piece I Place My Stones, created in collaboration with Arike, a musician and Cloud Blumstein, a dance artist. It was premiered at Battersea Arts Centre earlier this year.

Theresa Turk's parents were Polish immigrants who settled happily in England. She writes "I became a doctor and with the support of my husband and two sons, combined and enjoyed family and professional life, first in full time General Practice and then psychotherapy. Since childhood poetry had been important to me and about fifteen years ago I began to write seriously."

Michelene Wandor is a poet, playwright, critic and musician. Her selected poems, Gardens of Eden were published in 1990. Her prolific work for radio includes dramatisations of Jane Eyre, The Mill on the Floss, Persuasion and The Jungle Book, which was a runner-up for a Writer's Guild Award. More recently, her play, Orlando and Friends, for which she also arranged the music, was broadcast on Radio 3.

Lyn S. Westerman is an ex-kibbutz member and is currently a tutor for the London School of Journalism,

Publicity Chair for the Women Writers' Network and a drama student. A number of her short stories and poems have been published and she is working on her third novel. Lyn is divorced with a teenaged daughter.

Julie Whitby was educated at Bedales and trained for the stage at Central. Her poetry has appeared in the T.L.S., the Independent, the Scotsman, Agenda, She, Spare Rib, Country Life and elsewhere. Her first collection, The Violet Room (Acumen Publications), was published in 1994, as was Outside the Chain of Hands which features her work.

Tamar Yoseloff's first collection, Fun House, was published by Slow Dancer in 1994. In 1991 she won the London Writers' Competition. Her poems appear in various journals and anthologies including the Forward Book of Poetry 1994. She is the founder of Terrible Beauty, a weekly poetry series in London.

Barbara A. Zanditon's background is the East Coast American Jewish intellectual liberal tradition plus religion. She writes " At my Bat Mitzvah I abandoned, or was abandoned by, God. Nonetheless being Jewish defines who I am. I joined a synagogue when my then three year old daughter came home from school enthusiastically telling me about the baby Jesus. I believe, perhaps insanely, that you can live a secular life, marry out, and still be Jewish."

ACKNOWLEDGEMENTS

For permission to reproduce some of the poems in this
anthology, acknowledgment is made to the following:

For Wanda Barford to Outposts and Voices (Israel); for
Nadine Brummer to Writing Women; for Tricia Corob to
Poetry Now and Camden Voices; for Ruth Fainlight to
Sinclair-Stevenson; for Elaine Feinstein to Carcanet; for
Adèle Geras to Staple and Vision On 1994; for Miriam
Halahmy to Staple and Hub Editions; for Tamar Hodes to
Virago and Keele University Press; for Sue Hubbard to
Enitharmon; for Lila Julius to Voices and the Jewish
Women's Literary Annual; for Lotte Kramer to Rockingham
Press, Poet and Printer Press and Hippopotamus Press; for
Rochelle Mass to Arc, Annual Journal of Israel Association
of Writers in English, Kibbutz Trends and Voices; for
Gerda Mayer to Poetry Matters. The Spectator, The
Observer, and Encounter; for Pamela Melnikoff to the
Jewish Chronicle; for Lilian Mohin to Onlywomen Press
and Virago; for Anne Ranasinghe to Triton College
International Poetry Contest and Ariel; for Eva Salzman to
Bloodaxe; for Elizabeth Sarah to Manna; for Myra Schneider
to the Jewish Quarterly, Enitharmon, and Writing Women;
for Anna Sotto to Voices; for Gloria Tessler to Poetry Now;
for Theresa Turk to the Jewish Quarterly and Outposts; for
Michelene Wandor to Century Hutchinson; for Julie Whitby
to Acumen Publications, Encounter, Big Little Poem Books
and The Good Society Review; for Tamar Yoseloff to Writing
Women. The title "The Dybbuk of Delight" is taken from
Lilith's Dance by Michelene Wandor.

GLOSSARY

Adamah	female of Adam, Hebrew feminine for earth (h)
Al dabri	don't speak (h)
Babushka	grandmother (r)
Baruch Haboh	welcome; lit: blessed be he who comes, said at the invocation to the prophet Elijah at Pesach (h)
Bitte	please (g)
Booba	gran'ma (y)
Cholent	a stew, cooked overnight for Shabbos (y)
Dagesh	a Hebrew diacritic (h)
Desaparacidos	the disappeared (s)
Die Juden sind wunderschön	the Jews are marvellous (g)
Gefilte fish	fish balls, boiled or fried (y)
Golem	a human image brought to life (y)
Haggadah	prayer book used at the Passover meal telling the story of the exodus (h)
Havdallah	ritual ceremony marking the end of the sabbath (h)
Hayah, hoveh, yihyeh l'olam, va'ed	He was, He is, He will be for ever and ever (h)
Intifada	Palestinian uprising (a)
Kaddish	prayer of mourning (h)
Kalati	my bride (h)
Ketubah	marriage document (h)
Kiddush	prayer of sanctification (h)
Kipa	skull-cap (h)
Kneidlach	dumpling (y)
Kuchen	cake (g)
Kubeh	Middle-Eastern speciality of meat balls (a)
Kvetch	complaint (y)
Ledor vador	from generation to generation (h)
Matzo	thin biscuit of unleavened bread traditionally eaten during Passover (h)
Ne'ila	the closing prayers on the Day of Atonement (h)
Paschal	connected to passover/easter-tide
Passover	festival celebrating the Jewish exodus from Egypt
Pesach	Hebrew term for passover (h)
Pulka	leg of chicken (y)
Sachertorte	rich chocolate cake served in Vienna's Hotel Sacher (g)
Schvartze	black man (y)
Shabbos	sabbath (h)
Shiva	mourning period (h)

Shul	synagogue (y)
Strudel	apple and raisin cake (g)
Tallith	prayer shawl (h)
Tefillin	phylacteries (h)
Timbrel	ancient oriental tambourine
Yahrzeit candle	Jewish mourning candle (y)
Yom Kippur	Day of Atonement (h)
Yiddish	language based on a mixture of German and Hebrew
Zeyde	gran'pa (y)
(a)	Arabic
(g)	German
(h)	Hebrew
(r)	Russian
(s)	Spanish
(y)	Yiddish